Assessment of Client Core Issues

RICHARD W. HALSTEAD

AMERICAN COUNSELING ASSOCIATION
5999 Stevenson Avenue
Alexandria, VA 22304
www.counseling.org

Assessment
of
Client Core
Issues

10 9 8 7 6 5 4 3 2 1

AMERICAN COUNSELING ASSOCIATION
5999 Stevenson Avenue
Alexandria, VA 22304

DIRECTOR OF PUBLICATIONS
Carolyn C. Baker

PRODUCTION MANAGER
Bonny E. Gaston

COPY EDITOR
Kay Mikel

EDITORIAL ASSISTANT
Catherine A. Brumley

Text and cover design by Bonny E. Gaston.

LIBRARY OF CONGRESS CATALOGING-IN-PUBLICATION DATA
Halstead, Richard W.
    Assessment of client core issues / Richard W. Halstead.
        p.   cm.
    Includes bibliographical references.
    ISBN-13: 978-1-55620-235-3 (alk. paper)
    ISBN-10: 1-55620-235-0 (alk. paper)
    1.   Counseling.   I.   Title.

BF637.C6H295 2006
158'.3—dc22   2006009720

Dedication

This book is dedicated to my first and always family with whom I shared my formative years: my mom, June; dad, Donald; and sisters, Cherie and Marylou. Together they provided a wonderful foundation upon which to build a life of meaning and purpose. This work is also dedicated to my family of choice, Linda, Ben, Lisa, Mia, and Bluza, with whom I share the present. My families have provided amazing opportunities for living a full life of learning, and I truly cherish the time I have shared with them.

Contents

Preface

Living a life that results in finding personal satisfaction can be a challenging endeavor. Even under the best of circumstances, an individual is bound to struggle to some degree with the stresses, strains, and pressures that arise as a result of everyday living. Under less favorable conditions, individuals can become overwhelmed by stressful challenges and begin to lose a grasp on life's more enjoyable aspects. It is the counselor's role to assist those who may be experiencing a whole host of difficulties that might arise from such circumstances. Among the many complex factors involved in the counseling process is accurately conceptualizing the underlying nature of the client's problem and designing an appropriate counseling plan to address the client's overall struggle.

Early in my counseling career I came to what I thought was an important realization. It had occurred to me that clients' problems could be roughly grouped into two categories. In the first category were clients who presented with problems resulting from some unexpected event or isolated situation. In these cases, the client usually presented with no remarkable problematic history. In the second category were clients who presented with problems that were more complex in nature and that reflected a larger set of significant patterns of problematic issues that reoccurred over time. A client in this second category would present problems that often had a historical context and could be traced to earlier points of that client's life.

Having these categories helped me establish a framework for understanding the nature of a client's presenting problem, but it did little to help me design effective interventions. I struggled to provide effective interventions for clients in either category. I would create counseling plans that included an array of traditional counseling interventions with mixed results. I spent most counseling sessions actively listening to clients telling me in great detail about how, at certain points in their lives, they felt sad, anxious, confused, helpless, hopeless, unloved, abused, or angry. Despite all of this information, I rarely felt able to more fully understand the central issue or issues that continually generated discomforts or problematic response behaviors. With no framework for understanding the deeper nature of a client's problems—what I refer to in this book as the client's core issues—I often missed the bigger picture of each client's struggle. Without a broad frame of reference to work from, I found myself initiating a counseling process that would falter and eventually stall. The important outcome goal of either consistently helping the client adjust to a crisis event (category 1) or change repetitive problematic life patterns (category 2) was rarely achieved. As a result, I often felt frustrated and unable to provide the best possible counseling services to clients. More important, the larger core issues with which clients struggled often remained unaddressed and, as a result, unresolved.

When providing clinical supervision to counseling interns later in my career, I would often ask, "So what do you think is really going on at the core of this client's struggle?" My question was, in part, aimed at getting counseling interns to think past the more situational surface aspects of a client's presenting problem and the observable symptoms associated with that presenting problem so that they might focus on deeper aspects of the whole person. The other reason for posing this question was an attempt to get a bit closer to what I felt was missing in my own work as a counselor, understanding the client's core issues. Although the interns' responses to my question varied, it was clear that these well-schooled and talented novice counselors did not have a framework for understanding their clients' core issues any more than I did.

The problem of identifying and working effectively with core issues is not limited to those who lack experience. I have come to believe that the problem is more systemic in nature. During my tenure as a college mental health counselor and later as a counseling center director, I had access to information on clients who had been hospitalized for inpatient treatment. In hospital settings, symptom classification via the *Diagnostic and Statistical Manual of Mental Disorders*, 4th edition, text revision, or *DSM-IV-TR* (American Psychiatric Association, 2000), was where client assessment and treatment planning started and, all too often, seemed to end. It was after one such hospital case conference that I began to wonder about the power of models used for conceptualizing how a client presents. It occurred to me that conceptual models strongly influence what clinicians look for and, as a result, see in a client's presentation. What if the counseling profession had developed a complete companion manual to the *DSM-IV-TR* that focused on something other than sets of psychiatric symptoms as a means for conceptualizing client problems?

Counselors should not ignore the fact that some individuals benefit greatly from interventions based on the medical model. We must respect the fact that symptoms associated with current classifications of psychiatric disorders are synonymous with human suffering and, as such, counselors need to attend to intervention strategies that enhance the likelihood of symptom reduction. I am not suggesting, therefore, that there is no place for medically based assessment and treatment as a primary or ancillary intervention in one's overall clinical practice. What I am suggesting is that conceptualizing client problems based on the *DSM-IV-TR* has limitations. Counselors can move beyond those limitations by employing alternative models for conceptualizing client problems, such as the client core issues model presented here.

A major contribution of the multicultural counseling movement has been to advance the notion that a wide variety of valid perspectives exist for constructing a view of the world. Each perspective includes a contextual basis for understanding the nature of self, the social and relational roles of others, and the world's natural order. Through exposure to these ideas, members of the counseling profession have learned that holding a singularly absolute view of the world limits and marginalizes the validity of others. With more than one model for understanding the nature of the world, counselors can begin to see and understand aspects of life that previously were invisible or incomprehensible. I contend that the very same principles apply to the diagnostic conceptualization and understanding of client problems. Having only one formalized framework for diagnosing the nature of client problems is tantamount to imposing a culture of pathology on every client who seeks counseling services. This form of clinical encapsulation serves neither the client nor the counseling profession well.

As I continued to work with clients and developed as a counseling supervisor, it became clear that my work would be enhanced if I could more adequately conceptualize a client's reported problem on a deeper and more personally meaningful level. My goal was to find a problem classification framework that would allow me to better understand the core elements of a client's struggle as opposed to limiting my assessment to sets of observable symptoms. The underlying question associated with this goal was, "What are the core issue factors responsible for establishing and maintaining problematic thoughts, feelings, behavior, and associated meanings in the client's life?" If I could assist clients in articulating their concerns, I believed I could help them form a deeper understanding of their own struggles through the discovery of the thematic threads that ran through various problematic situations. If these thematic threads of a client's core issues could be identified, they would serve as working reference points from which new and perhaps more adaptive personal perspectives could be generated. The motivation for developing such an approach rested fully on the desire to bring resolution to the client's presenting concern and at the same time offer a means for helping the client create lasting change.

Using a client core issues framework has four advantages. First, such a framework allows the counselor to conduct an accurate assessment of the client's stated concern and draw some preliminary hypotheses about the core elements that may underlie the client's struggle. Second, once identified, the client's core issue becomes a focal point for designing an effective counseling plan and choosing appropriate interventions. Third, the counselor is better able to systematically monitor the client's progress in making transformational change over the course of the counseling process. Fourth, by committing a portion of the counselor's clinical focus to the client's core issue, the counselor helps facilitate the type of change that decreases the likelihood of relapse (Young, Beck, & Weinberger, 1994).

I believe that relational themes at the center of the client's problem are clinically richer and provide a more useful nomenclature than the classification of symptoms associated with psychiatric disorders. It is my contention that a different problem nomenclature provides a basis for forming a clearer understanding of the core nature or essence of a client's problem-based struggles as well as the accompanying symptoms. Using this different, and more expansive, understanding of diagnostic assessment, counseling intervention strategies can be designed to assist the client in making core changes that are more adaptive over the longer term. Put simply, this book has been written to help the counselor formulate an understanding of the client that is qualitatively different from the traditional psychiatric diagnosis. My hope is that the client core issues model will help counselors understand the core elements of the client's presenting problem and design appropriate interventions to help the client create lasting change.

OVERVIEW OF THE BOOK

In writing this book, I have drawn heavily on the creative ingenuity of others who have advanced theoretical perspectives in cognitive and narrative therapies. My contribution is in offering a unique integration and synthesis of these theoretical perspectives that can enhance a counselor's work with clients. As such, I have made every effort to present the ideas and concepts in a concise manner that lends itself well to clear clinical application for the practicing counselor or counseling student.

Chapter 1 sets the stage for considering alternatives to assessing a client's presenting problem and the client's responses to the stated struggles. Chapter 2 offers a theoretical overview of the proposed diagnostic framework, tracing the conceptual framework of the core issues model and the validity of the construct and describing the 18 core issues and their specific origins. Chapter 3 focuses on client core issues and the nature of the client's living story. Chapter 4 frames the thematic nature of core issues and how they are expressed as a living story detailed in a client's relational history and current life. Chapter 5 is a case study that illustrates how core issues are assessed, how the client's living story can be deconstructed to reduce the hold it has on the client's relational worldview, and how to help the client find specific themes around which a new, more adaptive living story can be created. A video of this case study is available through ACA Online Courses (www.counseling.org). Chapter 6 explains how counselors can begin to incorporate the proposed framework in their practice and assist their clients' in developing greater resourcefulness in coping with their difficult personal struggles as well as creating positive and lasting change in their lives.

Acknowledgments

I have drawn on the creative works of many scholars, past and present, who have developed better methods for helping others and published their theoretical perspectives and research findings. Most notably I have drawn on the work of Jeffery Young, PhD, who built on earlier theoretical concepts to propose a cognitively oriented and relationally based diagnostic framework.

More personally, a number of friends and colleagues have provided valuable suggestions, ideas, and encouragement. Special thanks are extended to Alan D. Goldberg, Syracuse University; John Derbort, COB Fellow; Marta Carlson, Assumption College; Pam Lizdas, Jody Farmer, Cindy Trifone, Judi Durham, Saint Joseph College; Amanda Costin, Cappella University; and Charlene Alderfer, College of New Jersey. In addition, I would like to extend my heartfelt gratitude to Carolyn Baker, Director of Publications at the American Counseling Association, for her time, attention, and patience. Finally, my special thanks to Linda Wagner who early on helped to stimulate my thinking and continued to support me in this endeavor.

About the Author

Richard W. Halstead graduated from high school in Auburn, New York, with a C average, a combined SAT score of 788, and in the bottom third of his graduating class. Prior to graduation, his high school counselor, Mrs. Flood, did her absolute best to discourage him from attending college for fear he was destined to suffer additional academic failure. Because his family lived and paid taxes within the city of Auburn, the community college in town, by policy, had to conditionally admit him for at least one semester, and they encouraged him to just give college a try. With his parents' support he took the risk of further humiliation in an academic setting and enrolled. Once exposed to college classes, he found the learning environment much better suited to his learning style and for the first time ever experienced a measured amount of academic success. Mrs. Flood passed away prior to his receiving a PhD, and Dr. Halstead stated, "Although the deaths of those who have played a role in one's life often bring sadness, in this particular case the timing of her passing was quite fortunate. Had she lived long enough to see me earn a doctoral degree, the shock of the event would most likely have killed her."

RICHARD W. HALSTEAD received a PhD in Counselor Education from Syracuse University. He is an associate professor and chair of the Department of Counselor Education at Saint Joseph College in West Hartford, Connecticut. Prior to joining the ranks of graduate counselor educators, he was the Director of Counseling and Student Development at Worcester Polytechnic Institute in Worcester, Massachusetts. He has published research articles on the nature of the counseling relationship and relationally based perspectives for engaging clients in processes of maturation and change. He was chosen by the students and faculty at Saint Joseph College to receive the John Stack Award for Excellence in Teaching in 2003.

CHAPTER 1

An Introduction to Client Core Issues

Linda, a 34-year-old biracial Amer-Asian woman, reports feeling sad and depressed. In her initial session she stated, "All the joy seems to have been drained out of my life." Although she is a well-paid and successful professional who has what she describes as very close friends, she struggles to "feel good" and rid herself of "feelings of being undesirable to others." As she reports her history, she becomes fully connected with the feelings she has held for many years about her father. Tearfully she reports that her military father left home when she was quite young. Although Linda feels her mother did a great job raising her as a single mother, she talks at length about how different her life would be if her father had been present while she was growing up.

Bill, an 18-year-old Caucasian man from an upper-middle-class family, presents with symptoms of depression. He is in the second semester of his freshman year in college and reports feeling very frightened about being alone. He cannot sleep because of intrusive thoughts that he will fail in school, and he worries that he is "going crazy." Even though Bill received very good grades in every course his first semester, he spends hours talking to his parents on the phone about how he cannot make it in college. Bill only feels comfortable when his father makes the 200-mile trip to visit him. At the time of intake, Bill gives his counselor permission to discuss anything and everything with his parents, whom he expects will be calling later in the day. Bill's father calls shortly after Bill's appointment. His father reports that he cannot believe that his son, "a very talented athlete," is calling home and crying about how scared he is about failing and being a disappointment. In an anxious and somewhat overbearing manner, his father says, "I have done everything for this kid. I have told him exactly what he needs to do every step of the way in order to be successful, and I was right there to make sure that he did it right. He is a very bright kid. His mother and I want the very best for him. Is it sports? Does he still like football? We will do anything for him. We just want him to be happy."

Ayesha, a 27-year-old African American woman, reports that she is "not doing well at all," explaining that another relationship she had hoped would lead to a life-long partnership ended about 3 months earlier. At the time of intake, Ayesha reported experiencing sleep disturbance, loss of appetite, anxiety, a lack of interest in socializing, a sense of hopelessness in her life, a decline of interest in her job (which she had previously enjoyed), and difficulty concentrating. Her symptoms have been present since the end of this most recent relationship, and she reports having experienced similar symptoms when previous relationships have ended. Ayesha explained, "It is always the same old thing. I work so hard to make a relationship work, and in the end it is all for nothing."

These three brief stories are typical of the struggles individuals bring to counselors. The basic steps of the counseling process include accurately assessing the nature of the client's problem, collaboratively agreeing on the goals of counseling, constructing a counseling plan, and implementing that plan to actualize the agreed upon outcomes. The work that the counselor and the client focus on is, to a great extent, determined by the manner in which the counselor goes about assessing, understanding, and defining the problematic nature of the client's struggle.

THINKING ABOUT CLINICAL DIAGNOSIS

The current standard for arriving at a clinical diagnosis in the mental health professions is generally through the use of the clinical interview. Typically, the counselor gathers information from the client and matches that information with a system of mental health nomenclature. The nomenclature system most widely used in the United States is the *Diagnostic and Statistical Manual of Mental Disorders,* 4th edition, text revision (American Psychiatric Association, 2000), or *DSM-IV-TR.* This medically based system of nomenclature has given practitioners and researchers a common language for labeling psychiatric disorders. It has also provided the clinician with three specific parameters for treatment. First, the system sets criteria for determining whether the diagnostic threshold for a particular psychiatric disorder has been met. Second, it provides the clinician with a set of target symptoms of interest to be reduced or alleviated during treatment. Third, it provides a set of symptom-based benchmarks against which the clinician can monitor the client's functioning (Shea, 1998).

In the past 20 years great strides have been made in establishing pharmaceutical and psychological treatment protocols aimed at controlling, reducing, or alleviating psychiatric symptoms as defined by the *DSM* system of nomenclature (Antony & Barlow, 2001; Levitt, Hoffman, Grisham, & Barlow, 2001). As helpful as the *DSM-IV-TR* is in providing a standard for the diagnosis and treatment of pathology, it presents the counselor with some inherent limitations.

The first *DSM* was published by the American Psychiatric Association in 1952. I began to wonder how the mental health field might be different today if the counseling profession had spent the last 54 years engaged in an effort to develop a classification system for understanding the core nature of client problems. If such a system had been developed, would today's counselors focus their attention and interventions on qualitatively different aspects of a client's reported difficulties? Would there be greater support for relational or human growth and development models of diagnosis and intervention? What if the counseling profession had developed a complete companion manual to the *DSM-IV-TR* that focused on something other than sets of psychiatric symptoms as a means for conceptualizing client problems? Would a system that focused on relationally based core problematic issues rather than on a set of psychiatric symptoms change the focus of a counselor's work with clients? Would having a framework that organized the basic thematic aspects of human difficulties serve to help form a better understanding of client responses to difficult struggles in life? My answer to all of these questions is an unqualified "yes"!

Using the *DSM-IV-TR* for Diagnosis

Typically, the basic elements necessary to reach a medically based diagnosis include the following:

- Type and frequency of symptoms associated with a particular syndrome
- Duration of those symptoms
- Medical conditions past and present that may suggest an organic cause for a disorder
- Type and intensity of life stressors present
- Level of impaired functioning at present and over the past year

Now consider the amount of information typically gathered in a thorough intake interview and compare it with that needed to render a medically based diagnosis. Much of information gathered at intake is not used in reaching a five-axis *DSM* diagnosis. Many dimensions of the client's life and history are not taken fully into account by the system of nomenclature used in a medically based diagnostic system. For example, detailed aspects of a client's family history, perceptions of self over time, spiritual beliefs, and meaning attached to life events are extremely rich inputs in constructing an understanding of the nature of the person and not just the disorder.

For the counselor who wishes to emphasize the nature of a client's experiential world and how it may relate to the client's problem, the nomenclature system embodied in the *DSM-IV-TR* falls short. Whether a client's symptoms meet the diagnostic criteria for a particular disorder, or the client reports some symptoms but not enough to meet the diagnostic threshold for a disorder, or the client presents a problem broad in nature that would normally be classified as a *DSM-IV-TR* V-code problem, the medically based system does not always serve counselors well (Kaslow, 1996; Kihlstrom, 2002). Put simply, a medically based system of nomenclature that emphasizes pathology does not provide the counselor with a systematic means for conceptualizing the core nature of a client's struggle. For example, the symptoms reported by Linda, Bill, and Ayesha at the beginning of this chapter could fit nicely into one of the categories of psychiatric disorders associated with depressive affective disorders. Knowing that a client is depressed, however, does not aid the counselor in developing a deeper understanding of the core issues that may be the source of a client's diagnostic symptoms. Much of the mental health profession has been built around the accurate classification of symptoms while assessment of the core nature of the client's life struggle is often left to little more than unstructured conjecture.

Even counselors schooled in the theoretical concepts of human growth and development who want to focus on the core issues central to a client's difficulty would be ill advised to do so without also including a medical model perspective for several reasons. First, some psychiatric disorders are tied to organic abnormalities and need to be treated medically. Second, accurately assessing the nature of any pathology a client may exhibit is valuable because it provides important reference points for further information gathering, establishing counseling goals, and constructing a counseling plan. Third, failure to establish a *DSM-IV-TR* assessment as a diagnostic reference point would surely bring questions about whether the counselor was fulfilling an ethical and legal responsibility to meet the standard of care established by the mental health profession (Corey, Corey, & Callanan, 2007; Madden, 1998). Fourth, any counselor who relies on a third party payor for the payment of fees must select a *DSM-IV-TR* diagnosis code. Therefore, even though the psychiatric nomenclature may not fit well with health, wellness, or a developmental frame of reference, counselors often must use the *DSM-IV-TR* nomenclature. As one counselor commented, "What are you going to do? It's the only game in town!" (M. L. Carlson, personal communication, September 21, 1996).

Limitations of the *DSM-IV* Assessment Model

Burke (1989) suggested that there is a basic dichotomy in working orientations for clinical intervention based on client need. The two categories in the dichotomy are (1) stabilization and reduction of client symptoms and (2) client growth and maturation. As one might surmise, each of these working orientations is associated with qualitatively different outcome goals.

The first category, stabilization and reduction of symptoms, is commonly associated with medically oriented models that conceptualize clients as struggling with pathological syndromes. The central questions asked in a medically based treatment orientation are as follows:

- What are the symptoms related to any particular diagnostic syndrome?
- What has been the duration of these symptoms?
- How can the specified symptoms be reduced to premorbid levels?

Applying this orientation to working with someone like Ayesha, the counselor knows that the client is depressed, that the symptoms have been present for 3 months, and that her depression is in response to the loss of a relationship with a potential life partner. Once the diagnosis has been made, the counselor has a specific set of symptom markers against which client progress can be tracked over the course of counseling. Some disorders correlate positively with certain risk concerns that the counselor should be certain to assess and continually monitor. In the case of a client diagnosed with severe depression, a counselor would surely want to make every effort to assess for suicidal ideation and recent actions that suggest the client is at risk of engaging in harmful behavior.

A close examination of the client stabilization or symptom reduction working orientation reveals some limitations to its usefulness. A first limitation is that not every client who seeks professional counseling services meets the criteria for a psychiatric disorder even though the client may be struggling with serious problems. In such cases the professional counselor is often left with no alternative nomenclature structure that can be used to systematically conceptualize the client's problems. The counselor who continues to think in terms of *DSM-IV-TR* diagnostic categories has two choices. First is the "close enough" approach. Even though the client's symptoms do not meet all the criteria for a particular disorder, the counselor uses the symptoms that are present to point in the direction of a specific diagnosis. In such cases the counselor might use terms such as "depressive-like presentation" or "some evidence of anxiety." The second choice is to look at the broader problem being presented and use the section of the *DSM-IV-TR* labeled "Other Conditions that May Be a Focus of Clinical Attention," commonly referred to as V codes. Categories such as Relationship Problem Not Otherwise Specified, Academic Problem, or Occupational Problem are so broad that they provide little help in arriving at a specific conceptualization of the problem let alone specific interventions to include in a counseling plan.

A second limitation of the *DSM-IV-TR* system is that it can be adopted as a generalized view of the world. The counselor begins to perceive a world where pathology abounds and understands every client as presenting with some form of pathology. When one is formally trained and experienced in the use of a classification system oriented toward the assessment and diagnosis of pathology, it is only reasonable to expect that pathology is indeed what one will recognize, assess, and ultimately diagnose. With no juxtaposing lens through which to view a client's struggle, the clinician can fall into the habit of pathologizing even normative responses to troubling life events. This concern is especially cautionary when framing pathology across cultures (Comas-Diaz, 1996); the variation in normative response must be understood relative to the client's worldview and the context of normative cultural life patterns and rituals.

A third limitation of this working orientation pertains to the treatment objectives associated with a stabilization and symptom reduction treatment frame. Although stabilization and symptom reduction are an important first phase of counseling, limiting outcome goals to reducing the symptoms associated with a particular disorder generally falls short of helping to foster the client's growth and development.

AN ALTERNATIVE DIAGNOSTIC FRAMEWORK

The second category of Burke's (1989) dichotomy of interventions is oriented toward client growth and maturation. The life-span development perspective serves as a hallmark for the counseling profession and has a very long history in the field of counseling (Barnes, 2003). By fostering the client's growth around a presenting problem or issue, the client will learn how to deal with similar problematic life issues differently, thereby reducing the likelihood of a relapse (Young, Beck, & Weinberger, 1994). The counselor choosing to work from a model that emphasizes human development must ask and answer a set of questions that is qualitatively different from those associated with a medically based treatment model. Whereas the medical model poses questions about the nature of the client's disorder syndrome, a growth-oriented model addresses a very different type of clinical challenge. Growth-oriented questions focus on the nature of the client and problematic relational patterns.

For example, a counselor working with Ayesha from a growth-oriented perspective would pose questions such as these: What factors have served to establish a pattern of failed relationships? Do Ayesha's series of failed relationships have elements in common? Why is Ayesha drawn to partners with whom she has to "work so hard"? Investigating questions like these, the counselor begins to address different dimensions of "the problem." Growth and development questions reveal aspects of the client's life that may not be congruent with the client's goals and may even reflect a problematic pattern that serves to keep the problem in place. In Ayesha's case, such questions can help to develop a better understanding of her relational worldview and can serve to reveal the elements that are at the core of her recurrent depressive episodes.

Posing client growth and maturation questions is not new. In some settings, these kinds of questions are quite common and often are part of a thorough psychosocial intake. It is unusual, however, for such questions and the information they generate to be used in a systematic manner as part of an integrated and structured diagnostic framework aimed specifically at assisting the clinician in forming a deeper understanding of a client's struggle. As Maslow (1971) warned, "If the only tool you have is a hammer, you tend to see every problem as a nail" (p. 56). It is time to seriously consider the manner in which members of the helping professions have been hammering away at clients' presenting issues via the classification of symptoms associated with frames of pathology. As Seligman and Csikszentmihalyi (2000) stated, "Treatment is not just fixing what is broken; it is nurturing what is best" (p. 7). To accomplish this goal, the counseling profession needs to offer counselors a different structural framework for assessing the nature of client problems and a different system of nomenclature for conceptualizing that with which the client struggles.

One might wonder how the field of counseling could have been enhanced if, in the early 1950s when the *DSM* was first published, the American Counseling Association (then the American Personnel and Guidance Association) had published a complementary diagnostic framework, perhaps a "Manual of Client Core Issues" (MCCI). This diagnostic guide would not have focused on symptoms of pathology but rather on psychosocial and relational formulations of client struggles that tend to be problematic in nature and impede a client's effort to experience more satisfaction in life. In all likelihood the MCCI would have gone through several revisions by now and perhaps be known today as the MCCI-IV. The framework advanced in such a guide would enable counselors to consider a complementary perspective and use it as an adjunct to the *DSM-IV-TR*. Such a guide would provide counselors with a systematic framework for assessing the different types of client core issues that tend to generate problematic responses to the troubling situations one faces in life. This framework would guide counselors in designing effective counseling interventions that address the sources of psychiatric symptoms as opposed to just categorizing these symptoms. This structure for understanding and placing core issues into a system of nomenclature would surely serve as an important addition to the current standards of practice in diagnosis and treatment.

A relationally based diagnostic framework was proposed by Young (1990), and subsequent refinements have produced a system of problem nomenclature that is widely applicable to the counseling profession (Young, Klosko, & Weishaar, 2003). The overall aim of presenting this model is to help counselors develop an understanding of what client core issues are, how they originate, and the role that a core issues perspective can play in helping to design and implement effective counseling strategies that result in lasting change. This approach to counseling requires counselors and clients to engage in a process of personal discovery and, ultimately, a process of growth. The clinical dimensions of this work include establishing a trusting relationship, becoming clear about the client's personal history, exploring the client's current and past relationship experiences, finding meaning in the client's responses to problems, and creating a vision for the client's future. This work also involves a specific process of first identifying and then exploring the elements of an individual's life that impede goal-congruent activities and how best to intervene in a manner that supports the client in achieving lasting change.

SUMMARY

As the field of counseling has broadened to meet the mental health needs of society in recent decades, there has been a steady move to conceptualize the nature of client problems with models that promote the diagnosis of pathology. The alignment of the counseling profession with psychiatry and clinical psychology has, in some ways, been a necessity as interdisciplinary treatment, managed care, and case law have all served to shape the current standard of care that counselors must meet. This alignment has also, unfortunately, limited how counselors assess clients' problems and design interventions that address core client issues as opposed to attending to the psychiatric symptoms associated with those issues.

CHAPTER 2

Conceptual Foundations for Understanding Client Core Issues

■

This chapter provides an overview of the core issues concept, a theoretical model for conceptualizing core issues, and an explanation of how core issues develop. A descriptive definition of each of the 18 core issue categories that comprise the model is provided in the chapter Appendix.

■

UNDERSTANDING CLIENT CORE ISSUES

Increased attention was given to the impact of acute traumatic events in the last half of the 20th century (Herman, 1992). Unfortunately, the necessity to attend to trauma continues. The destruction of the World Trade Center and the attack on the Pentagon, the impact of injury and death resulting from the Afghanistan and Iraq military conflicts, increases in domestic and urban violence, and the devastation in the wake of hurricanes Katrina and Rita have all contributed to the need for greater attention to counseling those exposed to trauma. Although trauma is a source of serious psychological and emotional problems, it is also important to recognize the impact of negative events, traumatic or not, that individuals experience over extended periods of time (Chu, 1992). Exposure to such events can create a host of difficult problems (Young, Beck, & Weinberger, 1994). Repeated losses, betrayals, or growing up under excessively rigid standards are just a few examples of the types of relational experiences that can have a profound impact on an individual's emotional world and become a source of psychological and emotional problems.

Negative problematic events may occur for many different reasons and can result in emotional wounds that last long after the experience itself has passed (Halstead, 1996). This is especially true for children, who often lack the personal power and skill to effectively change the environment in which they live. Individuals who cannot change a negative situation or remove themselves from that environment must find effective means for coping, which Lazarus (1991) defines as the "cognitive and behavioral efforts to manage specific external or internal demands that are appraised as taxing or exceeding the resources of the person" (p. 112).

The coping process first proposed by Lazarus and Folkman (1984) and elaborated further by Lazarus (1991) is shown in Figure 2.1. The model holds that a set of goal commitments, beliefs, and a base of knowledge come together to form the basic nature of an individual. These components include many aspects, from beliefs and individual preferences to temperament and character. The individual uses these components to assess the nature of specific situational conditions. When a situation arises, the individual will respond first by conducting what Lazarus and Folkman (1984) referred to as a "primary appraisal," analyzing the nature of the environmental stimulus and determining whether it is consistent with the individual's goal commitments, beliefs, and knowledge. In this way, the individual is construing the basic nature of the situation and the degree to which it is a threat. During primary appraisal, the individual asks, "What is the nature of this situation, and is it a threat to me or to the goals to which I am committed?"

FIGURE 2.1

Stress/Threat Model of Coping

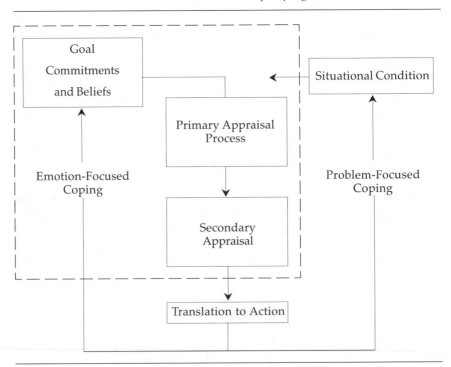

Note. From Lazarus & Folkman (1984); Lazarus (1991).

If the situational condition is assessed as a threat, the individual moves to the second step in the process. In secondary appraisal the individual assesses the resources he or she possesses to deal with the situational condition (Lazarus & Folkman, 1984). This is a kind of personal inventory of skills and abilities as well as social support resources. Secondary appraisal is directed toward determining how best to handle the threat that is being presented. The secondary appraisal process also involves individually specific action tendencies, affect, and the physiological responses experienced by the individual in response to the threat. These elements come together to determine the specific coping action the individual will employ.

Two forms of coping behavior are available, and both have the goal of minimizing distress associated with a problematic situational condition from the environment (Lazarus, 1991; Lazarus & Folkman, 1984). *Problem-focused coping* is directed outward: the goal is to change the situational conditions in the environment to reduce the negative impact experienced by the individual. Problem-focused coping is used when the individual believes his or her personal resources can be applied to change or reduce the impact of the situational condition. If successful, problem-focused coping modifies or alleviates the stressful or threatening nature of the situational condition.

In some cases efforts to change the impact of the situational condition directly fail to bring about the desired result of reducing or alleviating the stressor. In other cases, an individual may determine that the resources needed to successfully deal with the situational condition are inadequate. In these instances the individual responds by initiating emotion-focused coping strategies. Emotion-focused coping efforts rely primarily on various psychological processes to manage the negative effects that the stressor is having on the individual. *Emotion-focused coping* is a psychologically active process (Lazarus, 1991) in which internal activities are mobilized in an attempt to minimize the effects of the unpleasant or threatening situational condition. According to Carver, Scheier, and Weintraub (1989), a number of emotion-focused coping strategies can be activated. Strategies such as planning, positive reinterpretation, and humor can help the individual deal more effectively with life stressors. Negative forms of emotion-focused coping include mental or emotional disengagement, behavioral disengagement, denial, venting emotions inappropriately, and focusing on negative emotional reactions.

Whether an individual uses positive or negative emotion-focused coping strategies, this form of coping requires that the individual make internal psychological and emotional adjustments. Emotion-focused coping strategies result in modifications to an individual's goal commitments, beliefs, and knowledge. When the stressful situational condition is relational in nature and pertains to important emotional needs, the emotion-focused modifications made will have a direct impact on the individual's perceptions about the self, others, and the world.

The Role of Core Emotional Needs

Erikson (1963) proposed a useful framework for examining core needs during eight psychosocial developmental stages. The first five stages address the basic needs of a child from birth through adolescence (see Table 2.1). Erickson held that if a child's caregivers foster the child's development in a positive manner the child will grow through the stages of psychosocial development in good stead. If, however, the child's psychosocial environment does not support the child's basic needs, the individual will experience difficulties.

Core issues are thought to form as a result of the child's emotional needs not being adequately met during the span of time from infancy through adolescence (Young et al., 2003). Staub (1999) discussed the nature of human behavior when the fulfillment of basic human needs is frustrated:

> We human beings have certain shared psychological needs that must be fulfilled if we are to lead reasonably satisfying lives: We need to feel secure; we need a positive identity; we need to feel effective and to have reasonable control over what is essential to us; we need both deep connections to other people and autonomy or independence; we need to understand the world and our place in it. (p. 183)

Young et al. (2003) outlined a set of five core emotional needs that individuals are able to meet by making adaptations to their environment. Table 2.2 lists these five core needs and the nature of the relational environment that would support those needs. There is a direct connection between an individual's basic core need and the relational environment to which the individual is exposed. This connection is key in that it establishes the relational nature of the core issues with which many clients struggle.

Tied closely to core emotional needs are the beliefs formed about the relational environment and the influence these beliefs have on the individual. Everly and Lating (2004) proposed a set of five core beliefs that frame the nature of the human character:

1. The importance of living in a fair and just world
2. The importance of attachment to and trusting in other persons
3. The importance of a physically safe environment
4. The importance of a positive identity (i.e., esteem and efficacy)
5. The belief in some overarching order to life (i.e., religion, spirituality, a defining order, or unifying paradigm)

TABLE 2.1

Psychosocial Stages and Basic Human Needs

Erikson's (1963) Stages	Age	Basic Needs
Trust vs. Mistrust	Birth to 1½ years	Safety and security
Autonomy vs. Doubt	1½ to 3 years	Confidence and freedom from critical review
Initiative vs. Guilt	3 to 6 years	Freedom to express in play
Industry vs. Inferiority	6 to 11 years	Sense of competence
Identity vs. Role Confusion	Adolescence	Definition of self

TABLE 2.2

Core Emotional Needs and Desired Environmental Support

Core Emotional Needs	Relational Environments That Support Core Needs
Secure attachment	Safe, stable, nurturing, and accepting
Autonomy, competence, identity	Initiates action without excessive critical review
Expression of needs and emotions	Needs and emotions are respected and validated
Spontaneity and play	Expression of thought, feelings, and behavior
Realistic limits and self-control	Respects others and establishes personal limits

These five core psychological beliefs constitute "an essential thread within the fabric of human personality" (p. 33).

The consistency and similarity of thought in the various core belief models is striking and supports the idea that there must be a favorable psychosocial environment associated with becoming a well-adjusted individual. Put simply, a child has core emotional and psychosocial needs that should be adequately met. Further, the degree to which these core emotional needs are met depends largely on the quality of relational interactions within the environment. Those relational encounters establish sets of beliefs about the child's relational world, and these sets of beliefs form the basis for determining the nature of the child's future relational interactions.

Core Emotional Needs and Culture

How universal is the core emotional needs concept? Extreme caution should be taken when applying any conceptual understanding across cultures or even when applying such a concept to all individuals in one culture. Counselors need to consider the degree to which any model used to formulate the nature of clients' problems may be culturally biased and support one particular worldview over another (Ibrahim, Roysircar-Sodowsky, & Ohnishi, 2001). This determination is important in that it will dictate the degree to which any form of knowing can be widely applicable in guiding a counselor's work with clients whose worldviews may differ as a result of cultural affiliation.

Reaching a conclusion regarding the etic or emic nature of any perspective can be difficult and requires the counselor to consider a variety of factors (Sue & Sue, 2003). For example, the need for attachment is presented as a core emotional need, and Grossmann, Grossmann, and Keppler (2005) have indicated that this is a universal phenomenon. The method and means for fulfilling the attachment need, however, vary widely across cultures. The challenge is to discover how needs are expressed and met within a client's particular cultural framework. In doing so the counselor may find a broader multicultural applicability of core emotional needs that can serve as a basis for understanding.

Core emotional needs thought to come into play later in a child's development are more controversial. Establishing autonomy and forming a personal identity have also been conceptualized as basic core emotional needs, but the degree of individualism or collectivism desired within specific cultural groups varies (Pedersen, 2001). Autonomy is often thought of as a developmental task most closely associated with European American cultures. However, as described by Young et al. (2003), autonomy does not necessarily equal an independent individualistic expression of self (see Table 2.2). Rather, the definition provides an option for considering a wide array of actions free of excessive criticism. Therefore, initiating autonomous action as a means of supporting or advancing the wishes of the collective group is just as valid as more individualistic expressions of autonomy. Focusing attention on how these concepts are expressed within different cultures allows for a broader applicability of the model. Doing so also decreases the likelihood of the counselor imposing culturally biased beliefs that result in a narrow understanding of the client and the constructs that serve as a foundation for the client's worldview and from which the client constructs the meaning of self, others, and the world.

CONCEPTUALIZING CLIENT CORE ISSUES

To understand the core issues framework and how the methodology can serve as an orienting reference point for addressing client problems, counselors must be familiar with the basic principles and constructs upon which this perspective is based. The foundation of this perspective rests on understanding the concept of cognitive schema and its implications for clinical assessment and intervention design.

The concept of schema has been used by a variety of disciplines to convey the idea of a specific organizational structural theme or framework (Young et al., 2003). In the field of cognitive psychology the term *schema* is defined as an information organizing structure used to establish meaning. Piaget (1969) discussed cognitive schema as the primary cognitive structures that determine how children process information differently as they progress through specific stages of cognitive development. This use of the schema construct in cognitive psychology set the stage for its application in cognitive therapy. In one of his earliest writings describing cognitive therapy and its application for the treatment of depression, Beck (1967) defined schema as a primary element that serves to frame an individual's perceptual reality:

> A schema is a structure for screening, coding, and evaluating the stimuli that impinge on the organism. It is the mode by which the environment is broken down and organized into its many psychologically relevant facets. On the basis of that matrix of schemata, the individual is able to orient himself [herself] in relation to time and space and to categorize and interpret experiences in a meaningful way. (p. 283)

Beck's definition of cognitive schema provided a means for conceptualizing the interaction between a client's active information processing interaction and the environment. Wadsworth (1971) suggested that an organized set of schema serve two functions. First, similar to Beck's formulation, schema serve the individual by providing a primary means for processing information related to an experience and thereby establishing the meaning of that experience. Second, cognitive schema provide the basis for formulating a response to the meaning that has been made from that experience.

Cognitive Schema and Worldview

Interestingly, the early works that popularized various forms of cognitive and cognitive behavioral approaches to counseling and therapy did not focus on such concepts as basic schema structure or schema-based information processing models of therapy. Rather, the early works focused on activating events, beliefs, automatic thoughts, internal dialogue, negative self-talk messages, maladaptive assumptions, and so forth (Beck, Rush, Shaw, & Emery, 1979; Beck & Young, 1985). According to Goldfried (2003), earlier cognitive interventions fell short of capturing the full picture of an individual's primary functioning and therefore generated interventions that were limited in scope and effectiveness. Goldfried pointed out that it was not until cognitive therapy moved away from focusing solely on secondary elements of client functioning and began focusing on the primary elements of meaning-making structures consistent with cognitive science that richer forms of therapeutic approaches advanced.

As the essential organizer of meaning, cognitive schema provide the conceptual framework for understanding how an individual establishes a worldview. Beck and Weishaar (1989) hypothesized that schema are developed during childhood and become increasingly elaborate as the individual gains life experience. A specific subset of relationally focused schema, usually established during childhood and adolescence, serve to filter and evaluate the nature of relationship encounters (Beck, 1967). It is this special subset of relational schema that is of most interest when considering client core issues. In fact, core issues result from an individual establishing maladaptive relational schema (Young, 1990). These maladaptive relational schema are the source of difficulties as individuals interact with the world and, therefore, are thought of as a first-order problem (Young et al., 2003). Early maladaptive schema constitute the core issues with which clients struggle. This particular class of schema generate the symptoms associated with many nonorganically based *DSM-IV-TR* Axis I diagnoses and character disorders diagnosed on Axis II.

Early Maladaptive Schema and Core Issues

Schema can be classified as either positive or negative. Positive schema organize meaning about the self, others, and the world in a variety of ways that are adaptive. Negative schema organize meaning in a manner that is maladaptive in the individual's current environment (Sharf, 2003).

Young (1990, 1999) advanced the idea that repetitive negative, toxic, or goal-incongruent experiences associated with trying to meet core emotional needs activate a special set of maladaptive schema. Because these negative experiences are formed within the context of relational interactions, the schema established around those relationships tend to skew an individual's relational worldview and result in a tendency for the individual to interact with others in a manner that impedes more adaptive functioning. Negative schema-based response tendencies may have been adaptive when core emotional needs were not being met in childhood and the child was powerless to change the relational environment (Young, 1990). As the individual grows and begins to move into other relational environments, however, the maladaptive relational worldview becomes problematic. Problems arise as maladaptive schema are triggered and lead to self-defeating cognitive, affective, and behavioral responses. Over time these self-defeating tendencies can become more generalized patterns of interaction that directly interfere with the individual's ability to fulfill specific needs, wants, and desires (Young, 1990, 1999). Young proposed that early maladaptive schema have a particular set of descriptive characteristics that can be used to assess the core elements that support problematic interactions in an individual's life.

According to Young, Klosko, and Weishaar (2003), the most recent formulation of early maladaptive schema consists of four broad descriptive elements. First, as previously stated, early maladaptive schema usually develop as a direct result of one or more core emotional needs that have not been met on a consistent basis in childhood or adolescence. Second, without intervention or some other corrective set of emotional experiences, early maladaptive schema are further refined and incorporated as part of the individual's relational worldview as that person moves through life. Third, early maladaptive schema suggest specific, relationally oriented themes or patterns that tend to be pervasive and can be traced over an individual's history. Fourth, when fully activated, these schema generate an associated set of intense cognitions, emotions, and behavioral responses that interfere with the individual meeting specific short- and long-term goals. For that reason, early maladaptive schema are thought to be dysfunctional.

Young's (1990, 1999) earliest formulations of early maladaptive schema were initially understood as the basic core issues related to personality disorders. Young proposed that this subset of relational schema could be used for both assessing the nature of particular personality disorders and designing more effective treatment for clients presenting with Axis II disorders. In response to additional research and clinical application of this framework, the utility of early maladaptive schema has been expanded to include not only personality disorders but also less severe character-related problems and Axis I psychiatric disorders (Ball, Mitchell, & Malhi, 2003; Cecero & Young, 2001; Flanagan, 1993; Hoffart, Versland, & Sexton, 2002; Lee, Taylor, & Dunn, 1999; Morrison, 2000; Schmidt, Joiner, Young, & Telch, 1995; Young & Flanagan,

1998; Young & Gluhoski, 1997; Young & Mattila, 2002; Young et al., 2003). This expansion in clinical application provides a valuable adjunct for counselors when conceptualizing the core nature of client problems. Conducting an assessment of early maladaptive schema provides a structured approach for arriving at the core issues that are the root cause of a client's distress. This form of assessment also provides a counselor with the means for extending problem conceptualization beyond a process of symptom classification and fosters interventions that support client growth as well as symptom reduction.

DEVELOPMENT OF MALADAPTIVE CORE ISSUES

Core issues are an artifact of an individual's acceptance of early maladaptive schema. Core issues are the primary problematic elements of an individual's intrapersonal and interpersonal meaning-making system that, when activated, serve to generate problematic responses to situational conditions over time. To more fully grasp the concept of core issues, it is helpful to examine each portion of the definition separately. The first element addresses the focus of a client's intrapersonal and interpersonal experience. The importance of this focus rests on an underlying contention that all problems clients present are, in one form or another, relationship problems (Carnevale, 1989). Think for a moment about the relational nature of an individual's life. It can be argued that an individual is constantly engaged in relationship. The form of relationship the individual engages in is dictated by qualitatively different relational dyads. These dyads, as depicted in Figure 2.2, are self in relationship with self, self in relationship with another or group, and self in relationship with the natural world. These three formulations of relational connection constitute a relational triad. Thinking about the nature of relationships enables the counselor to better analyze those aspects of the problem with which the client is struggling and the intrapersonal or interpersonal dynamics of that struggle.

The relational triad allows the counselor to classify three basic problem situations, each of which reflects a relational core issues perspective. These three basic relationally based problems follow the points contained in the relational triad and include (1) relational problem with self, (2) relational problem with other, and (3) relational problem with the nature of the world (Burke,

FIGURE 2.2

Elements of the Relational Triad

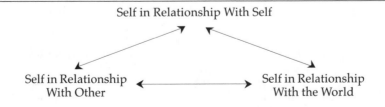

1989; Carnevale, 1989). Clients' relational issues can be found somewhere along the continuums shown in Figure 2.3.

The first two forms of relational problems are fairly straightforward. Relationship-with-self problems exist somewhere along a continuum expressed at the extremes as "I hate myself" or "I love my self to the exclusion of others." The further one moves toward either end of the continuum, the more difficult one's experience often is. Relationship-with-other problems also exist along a continuum with the poles consisting of "I am not getting what I want or need from others" (emotional support, empathy, love, and so forth) or "I am getting what I do not want or need from others" (physical mistreatment, verbal abuse, emotional abuse, overprotection, smothering, and so forth). The third form of relationship is one's relationship to the nature of the world. The continuum poles for this dimension consist of "I am not getting what I want or need from the world" (goal-congruent events) and "I am getting what I do not want or need from the world" (goal-incongruent events).

Unlike the first two types of relationally oriented problems, the third type is less commonly addressed and perhaps best explained through the use of an example. About a year ago a colleague of mine who had always been very physically active and enjoyed a variety of outdoor activities was diagnosed with multiple sclerosis. His immediate response was how unfair it was for him to have to deal with this disease. His initial emotional response was a great deal of intense anger. This anger was not directed at himself or any individual in his life but rather at the seemingly cruel nature of how the world works. At times it is the randomness of natural occurrences in life that can become the source of a problem to which an individual will then respond.

For some clients, "relationship with the nature of the world" category problems may also be expressed in spiritual terms. In such cases the counselor may do well to listen for references to a deity that is understood by the client to have power over all aspects of life. Listening for the client's point of relational reference as the problem is initially presented can be tremendously useful in that it provides an initial means for defining the nature of the client's presenting concern.

FIGURE 2.3

Use of the Relational Triad for Problem Analysis

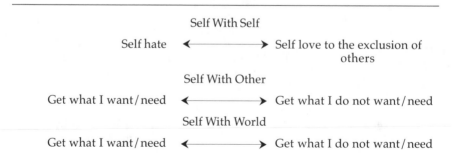

Self With Self

Self hate ←——————→ Self love to the exclusion of others

Self With Other

Get what I want/need ←——————→ Get what I do not want/need

Self With World

Get what I want/need ←——————→ Get what I do not want/need

The second portion of the core issues definition holds that core issues are activated or triggered and come into play under certain interpersonal or intrapersonal conditions or circumstances. When core issues are activated, they tend to generate problematic responses. The schema to which the core issue is related will generate automatic thoughts, strong affect, and behavioral tendencies that tend to be maladaptive in nature (Young, 1990, 1999).

The third element in the definition of core issues is the idea that the client's responses tend to be evident over time. If the client is indeed struggling with one or more core issues, it would make sense that patterns of responses consistent with these problems could be traced back over time. Without appropriate intervention, it is likely that the pattern will continue into the future.

Young's Schema Domains

Identification of the core needs that were not sufficiently met at an early point in the client's life is a key element in both assessing the nature of a client's core issue and in designing appropriate interventions. According to Young (1990, 1999; Young et al., 2003), each of the five basic core emotional needs is associated with a different broad schema domain. Table 2.3 shows the connection between the five core human needs and the five broad schema domains with which each is associated.

The first schema domain is Disconnection and Rejection. This domain reflects a relational environment in which caregivers are not reliable in providing the core emotional needs of safety, security, love, and companionship. As a result, the individual forms a worldview that relationships are unstable and that others will tend to disconnect or be rejecting.

The second schema domain, Impaired Autonomy and Performance, is characterized by a relational environment that supports forms of emotional enmeshment or intrapersonal and interpersonal restraint. The core emotional needs at issue here are personal autonomy, competence, and a sense of identity. In this environment the individual receives messages that survival and well-being are not possible without continual guidance, direction, and advice.

TABLE 2.3

Core Emotional Needs and Schema Domains

Core Emotional Need Not Met	Associated Maladaptive Schema Domain
Secure attachment to others	Disconnection and Rejection
Autonomy, competence, and sense of identity	Impaired Autonomy and Performance
Realistic limits and self-control	Impaired Limits
Freedom to express valid needs and emotions	Other-Directedness
Spontaneity and play	Overvigilance and Inhibition

The third schema domain, Impaired Limits, reflects the types of issues that arise when an individual has not learned to discern realistic limits and exercise self-control. Individuals who experience difficulties related to this domain have observed a relational environment wherein limits are either overly rigid or overly lax in some respect. These individuals have trouble either responding adequately to the needs of others or fulfilling their own needs.

The fourth schema domain, Other-Directedness, is characterized by an excessive emphasis on fulfilling the wants or emotional needs of others to an extent that it becomes detrimental to one's self. Issues within this domain arise when the relational environment does not support or validate the importance of the individual's needs and emotions. To get emotional needs met, or at the very least avoid another's anger, an individual in this environment remains constantly available to others to meet their needs rather than his or her own.

Overvigilance and Inhibition, the fifth schema domain, addresses the basic needs for pleasure, happiness, spontaneity, and expression. If an individual's relational environment inhibits opportunities to experience happiness, a worldview without any sense of joy or pleasure may develop.

Maladaptive Relational Schema

It is important to focus on the broad nature of the maladaptive schema domain during the initial phase of assessment (Young, 1990, 1999). First, noting the schema domain helps to define the broad categories of the client's struggle. Second, each domain characterizes the broad goals the client is striving to accomplish. Third, knowing the schema domain provides a direction for achieving the broad goal of counseling, helping the client overcome the maladaptive schema. Once the schema domain is identified, the counselor can focus on the specific early maladaptive schema that are at work as core issues in the client's life.

Recall once again how Young (1990, 1999) formulated the concept of early maladaptive schema core issues: core issues form when the individual encounters relational interactions that fail to meet one or more core emotional needs on a continuous basis. These relational encounters are, in essence, repeated relationally oriented stressful situational conditions with which an individual must cope. If the necessary resources in problem-focused coping are available to change the nature of the situational condition, it is likely that there will be little lasting impact on the individual (Lazarus, 1991). However, an individual without access to these resources or the power to engage successfully in problem-solving coping must employ emotion-focused coping.

Early and continuous relationship encounters characterized by extremes have a severe impact on a client's perception of the world. When the only response to maladaptive relational interactions is to continually engage in emotion-focused coping, the individual's relational view of self, others, and the world will reflect those experiences (Lazarus, 1991). The case example that follows illustrates how this coping process serves to create an individual's core issues.

The Case of John

John, 13 years of age, is the oldest of three children. His mother and father both work and do not get home until after six in the evening. John just completed an in-school babysitting course and holds a babysitting certificate, which is required by law in his state for any child over the age of 12 to provide babysitting services. John hoped he could earn extra money babysitting for families in his neighborhood, but now that his parents can legally leave him to babysit, John is responsible for watching his two younger siblings, starting dinner, and doing household chores after school. John dislikes this situation because he cannot join friends after school for play and sports activities. Because of his work responsibilities in the home environment, John's core emotional needs for spontaneity and play are being restricted.

In response to this situational condition, John's coping process is activated in the following manner. A situational condition, in this case being held responsible for family tasks, exists as a stressor in John's life. He begins the coping process by first cognitively construing the nature of the situational condition. The way a situation is construed depends largely on aspects of personality, goal commitments, beliefs, and knowledge (Lazarus, 1991). John construes the nature of this situational condition as being incongruent with his goals of interacting with his friends and engaging in after-school activities that are more to his liking. Next, John enters into a secondary appraisal process, assessing the personal and social resources available to him in responding to the situation. John will become aware of experiential outcomes, including certain action tendencies, affect responses, and physiological experiences. Feeling angry and frustrated, John now moves to coping options.

At this point in his life, John has experienced a fair amount of success dealing with environmental stressors head on. His secondary appraisal translates into taking the action of problem-solving coping with the hope that, if successful, the stressful situational condition will be alleviated. When his parents arrive home from work, John launches into an angry protest about having to be at home when his friends are outside enjoying the after-school hours. John's parents are unmoved by his protest. They explain that everyone in the family is expected to make a contribution and that at 13 years of age he needs to help in the family effort. John protests and argues further, but his parents hold fast to their position.

Because John was not successful in his attempts to change the situation and the situation remains a present stressor, John must now employ emotion-focused coping strategies. Engaging in emotion-focused coping requires the individual to rely on active internal psychological processes. John will mobilize his emotion-focused coping strategies to manage the cognitive, emotional, and physiological responses to the situational condition that he has appraised as a threat.

John's situation is far from a worse case scenario. In fact, it might be viewed by some as an important character-building milestone that supports meeting one's responsibilities and the meaning of contributing to the family. Others might argue that by placing too much responsibility on John, his parents are restricting his ability to develop normative peer relationships that evolve from after-school activities. In either case, the process of emotion-focused coping impinges on John's beliefs, goal commitments, and knowledge about self, others, and the world. If exposed repeatedly to similar stressful relational encounters, John's pattern of emotion-focused coping will, over time, reshape the relational schema that serve to organize his relational worldview.

■

Some children are forced to endure much greater hardship. Emotion-focused coping strategies are often employed by children living in environments in which there is continual abuse, abandonment, or overprotection, or in which the children are held to unrelenting high standards. A child consistently treated in these ways will naturally form relational schema that are consistent with the nature of the mistreatment. The relational schema that are formed and serve to order the child's relational worldview will reflect the negative relational experiences that are perpetuated in these less than ideal environments. Schema formed within the context of negative relational experiences will reflect the dysfunctional nature of that environment. The worldview that is constructed from these schema is decidedly negative, and difficulties are almost certain to occur when an individual's interactions are informed by these negative schema. The appendix to this chapter describes the specific core issues associated with the five schema domains.

SUMMARY

This chapter addressed the fundamental concepts upon which the core issues perspective has been built. Repeated exposure to relational environments in which core emotional needs are not adequately met result in emotion-focused coping. Core issues develop as this patterned behavior continues. Cognitive schema establish how the individual organizes meaning regarding relationship with self, relationship with others, and relationship with the world. When the relational environment fails to provide for core emotional needs, maladaptive relational schema are formed. These maladaptive schema, when triggered, organize information in a manner that results in particular thoughts, feelings, and behaviors that tend to be problematic in an individual's current relational interactions. Chapter 3 builds on the principles presented thus far and examines the elements involved in conducting a core issues assessment.

Disconnection and Rejection
(Expectation that one's needs for security, safety, nurturance, empathy, sharing of feelings, acceptance, and respect will not be met in a predictable manner. Typically family of origin is detached, cold, rejecting, withholding, lonely, explosive, unpredictable, or abusive.)

1. *Abandonment/Instability.* The perceived instability of those available for support and connection. Involves the sense significant others will not be able to continue to provide emotional support, connection, strength, or practical protection because they are emotionally unstable and unpredictable (for example, angry outbursts), unreliable, or erratically present; because they will die imminently; or because they will abandon the client in favor of someone better.

2. *Mistrust/Abuse.* The expectation that others will hurt, abuse, humiliate, cheat, lie, manipulate, or take advantage of the individual. The schema usually involves the perception that the harm is intentional and is the result of unjustified and extreme negligence. It may include the sense that the individual always ends up being cheated relative to others or "getting the short end of the stick."

3. *Emotional Deprivation.* The expectation that the individual's desire for a normal degree of emotional support will not be adequately met by others. The three major forms of emotional deprivation are as follows:

    A. Deprivation of nurturance: absence of attention, affection, warmth, or companionship

    B. Deprivation of empathy: absence of understanding, listening, self-disclosure, or mutual sharing of feelings from others

    C. Deprivation of protection: absence of strength, direction, or guidance from others

4. *Defectiveness/Shame.* The feeling that the individual is inwardly defective, bad, unwanted, inferior, or invalid in important respects; or that the individual would be unlovable by significant others if exposed. This schema may involve hypersensitivity to criticism, rejection, and blame; self-consciousness, comparisons, and insecurity around others; or a sense of shame regarding perceived flaws. These flaws may be private (for example, selfishness, angry impulses, unacceptable sexual desires) or public (for example, undesirable physical appearance, social awkwardness).

5. *Social Isolation/Alienation.* The feeling that the individual is isolated from the rest of the world, is different from other people, or is not part of any group or community. This schema has to do more with how a client feels in a group rather than when with those who have established emotional ties.

Impaired Autonomy and Performance
(Expectations about self and the environment that interfere with the individual's perceived ability to separate, survive, function independently, or perform successfully. Typically from a family of origin that is enmeshed or undermines child's confidence, is overprotective, or fails to reinforce the child for performing competently outside the family.)

6. *Dependence/Incompetence.* Belief that the individual is unable to handle everyday responsibilities in a competent manner without considerable help from others (for example, take care of self, solve daily problems, exercise good judgment, tackle new tasks, make good decisions). A client with this core issue will often present as helpless.

7. *Vulnerability to Harm or Illness.* Exaggerated fear that imminent catastrophe will strike at any time and that the individual will be unable to prevent it. Fears focus on one or more of the following: (a) medical catastrophes such as heart attacks or AIDS; (b) emotional catastrophes such as "going crazy"; or (c) external catastrophes such as elevators collapsing, criminal victimization, airplane crashes, or earthquakes.

8. *Enmeshment/Undeveloped Self.* Excessive emotional involvement and closeness with one or more significant others (often parents) at the expense of full individuation of normal social development. Often involves the belief that at least one of the enmeshed individuals cannot survive or be happy without the constant support of the other. May also include feelings of being smothered by, or fused with, others, or insufficient individual identity. Often experienced as a feeling of emptiness and floundering, having no direction, or in extreme cases questioning one's existence. The parent often merges with the child and tries to limit differences between them. The child grows into an adult with a sense that he or she cannot function without the person with whom the child is enmeshed. The parent's message very likely was, "We are one person, and we must always be together." This creates a tremendous sense of guilt when the child has to separate. The client lives an existence that is largely an extension of the parent.

9. *Failure.* The belief that the individual has failed, will inevitably fail, or is fundamentally inadequate relative to peers in areas of achievement (school, career, sports, and so forth). Often involved beliefs that the individual is stupid, inept, untalented, ignorant, lower in status, or less successful than others.

Impaired Limits
(Deficiency in internal limits, responsibility to others, or long-term goal orientation. Leads to difficulty respecting the rights of others, cooperating with others, making commitments, or setting and meeting realistic personal goals. Typical family of origin is characterized by permissiveness, overindulgence, lack of direction, or a sense of superiority—rather than appropriate confrontation, discipline, and limits in relation to taking responsibility, cooperating in a reciprocal manner, and setting goals. In some cases, the child

may not have been pushed to tolerate normal level of discomfort or may not have been given adequate supervision, direction, or guidance.)

10. *Entitlement/Grandiosity.* The belief that the individual is superior to other people; is entitled to special rights and privileges; or is not bound by the rules of reciprocity that guide normal social interaction. Often involves insistence that the individual should be able to do or have whatever he or she wants, regardless of what is realistic, what others consider reasonable, or the cost to others; or an exaggerated focus of superiority (for example, being among the most successful, famous, or wealthy to achieve power and control, not primarily for attention of approval). Sometimes includes excessive competitiveness toward, or domination of, others: asserting power, forcing one's point of view, or controlling the behavior of others in line with one's own desires without empathy or concern for others' needs and feelings.

11. *Insufficient Self-Control/Self-Discipline.* Pervasive refusal to exercise sufficient self-control and self-discipline; low frustration tolerance to achieve personal goals; lacking restraint from excessive expression of emotions and impulses. In it milder form, the client presents with an exaggerated emphasis on discomfort avoidance: avoiding pain or conflict, confrontation, responsibility, or overexertion at the expense of personal fulfillment, commitment, or integrity.

Other-Directedness

(An excessive focus on the desires, feelings, and responses of others at the expense of the individual's own needs to gain love and approval, maintain one's sense of connection, or avoid retaliation. Usually involves suppression and lack of awareness regarding one's own anger and natural inclinations. Typically, the family of origin is based on conditional acceptance: children must suppress important aspects of themselves to gain love, attention, and approval. In many such families, the parents' emotional needs and desires— or social acceptance and status—are valued more than the unique needs and feelings of each child.)

12. *Subjugation.* Surrendering control to others because one feels coerced— usually to avoid anger, retaliation, or abandonment. Usually involves the perception that one's own desires, opinions, and feelings are not valid or important to others. Frequently presents as excessive compliance combined with hypersensitivity to feeling trapped. Generally leads to a buildup of anger, which is manifested in maladaptive symptoms (passive-aggressive behavior, uncontrolled outbursts or temper, psychosomatic symptoms, withdrawal of affection, "acting out," or substance abuse). The two major forms of subjugation are as follows:

A. Subjugation of needs: suppression of one's preference, decisions, and desires

B. Subjugation of emotions: suppression of emotional expression, especially anger

13. *Self-Sacrifice.* Excessive focus on voluntarily meeting the needs of others in daily situations at the expense of the individual's own gratification. The most common reasons are to prevent pain to others; to avoid guilt from feeling selfish; or to maintain the connection with others as needy. Often results from an acute sensitivity to the pain of others. Sometimes leads to the sense that one's own needs are not being adequately met and to resentment of those who are taken care of. (Overlaps with the concept of codependency.)
14. *Approval Seeking.* Excessive emphasis on gaining approval, recognition, or attention from other people, or fitting in, at the expense of developing a secure and true sense of self. One's sense of esteem is dependent primarily on the reaction of others rather than on one's own natural inclinations. Sometimes includes an overemphasis on status, appearance, social acceptance, money, or achievement as means of gaining approval, admiration, or attention (not primarily for power and control). Frequently results in inauthentic or unsatisfying major life decisions or in hypersensitivity to rejection.

Overvigilance and Inhibition
(Excessive emphasis on suppressing one's spontaneous feelings, impulses, and choices or on meeting rigid internalized rules and expectations about performance and ethical behavior—often at the expense happiness, self-expression, relaxation, close relationships, or health. Typical family of origin is grim, demanding, and sometime punitive: Performance, duty, perfection, following rules, hiding emotions, and avoiding mistakes predominate over pleasure, joy, and relaxation. There is usually an undercurrent of permission and worry that things could fall apart if one fails to be vigilant and careful at all times.)

15. *Negativity and Pessimism.* A pervasive and lifelong focus on the negative aspects of life (pain, death, loss, disappointment, conflict, guilt, resentment, unsolved problems, potential mistakes, betrayal, events that could go wrong, and so forth) while minimizing or neglecting the positive or optimistic aspects of life. Usually includes an exaggerated expectation—in a wide range of work, financial, or interpersonal situations—that things will eventually go seriously wrong or that aspects of one's life that seem to be going well will ultimately fall apart. Usually involves an inordinate fear of making mistakes that might lead to financial collapse, loss, humiliation, or being trapped in a bad situation. Because potential negative outcomes are exaggerated, these clients are frequently characterized by chronic worry, vigilance, complaining, or indecision.
16. *Emotional Inhibition.* The excessive inhibition of spontaneous action, feeling, or communication—usually to avoid disapproval by others, feelings of shame, or losing control of one's impulses. The most common areas of inhibition involve (a) inhibition of anger; (b) inhibition of positive impulses such as joy, affection, sexual excitement,

and play; (c) difficulty expressing vulnerability or communicating freely about one's feelings or needs; or (d) excessive emphasis on rationality while disregarding emotions.

17. *Unrelenting Standards.* The underlying belief that one must strive to meet very high internalized standards of behavior and performance, usually to avoid criticism. Typically results in feelings of pressure or difficulty slowing down and in being hypercritical toward oneself and others. Must involve significant impairment in pleasure, relaxation, health, self-esteem, sense of accomplishment, or satisfying relationships. Unrelenting standards typically present as (a) perfectionism, inordinate attention to detail, or an underestimate of how good one's own performance is relative to the norm; (b) rigid rules and "shoulds" in many areas of life, including unrealistically high moral, ethical cultural, or religious precepts; or (c) preoccupation with time and efficiency so that more can be accomplished.

18. *Punitiveness.* The belief that people should be harshly punished for making mistakes. Involves the tendency to be angry, intolerant, punitive, and impatient with people (including oneself) who do not meet one's expectations or standards. Usually includes difficulty forgiving mistakes in oneself or others because of a reluctance to consider extenuating circumstances, allow for human imperfection, or empathize with the feelings of others.

From "Depression," by J. E. Young, A. Weinberger, & A. T. Beck. In *Clinical handbook of psychological disorders*, D. H. Barlow (Ed.), 2001 (3rd ed., pp. 271–273). New York: Guilford Press. Reprinted with permission.

CHAPTER 3

Assessment of Core Issues
and the Nature of the Client's Living Story

Conducting a good assessment requires applying a number of counseling skills in a methodical manner. If the assessment is successful, the counselor will be able to formulate a clear conceptualization
of the client, the nature of the client's problem, and the root cause
of that problem. Because clients often present with difficulties that
are layered in complex ways, establishing a basic understanding
of where to begin and what is important to focus on can be a major
challenge. Consider the following story.

A number of years ago, while a graduate student, I was involved in a supervision group session with my primary supervisor and two other counseling
interns. It was early in the semester, and this was the first time I was to present
a client I had met with the previous day for an intake interview. In reporting
the client's early history, I used a standard statement I had seen many times
in textbooks: "This client seems to have had a very normal childhood with
no remarkable emotional or psychological events." Upon hearing my statement the supervisor held up his hand, stopping me from sharing my next
piece of information. As I was about to find out, this particular supervisor
was extremely skilled at creating intense learning experiences in supervision. He was a master at composing a moment within which important learning would take place in a manner that often had a profound impact on his
supervisees. In this instance, he paused for what seemed like a very long
time and looked straight at me with a locked gaze. I could feel myself becoming tense and was not sure what it was that had caught his attention. The
other interns looked down at the floor to avoid drawing any attention to themselves. Then, in a voice barely audible, my supervisor said, "Childhood, no
matter how normal it may appear, is always a difficult emotional and psychological struggle. Each of us who has made it to adulthood has had to

survive childhood. It is your job to help the client give a voice to the experience of that struggle" (J. R. Wilett, personal communication, September 1985). He then sat silently for another moment, creating space for his statement to have its full affect.

Messages delivered at moments like that have a way of staying with a counselor for a long time. That message was largely responsible for helping me to realize the value of applying the core issues framework in working with clients. Assessing the nature of a client's core issues helps the counselor to define the material that is most important and on which the counseling intervention should be based.

DEVELOPMENTAL FACTORS

Central to the human experience is the range of experiences associated with relational connectedness to self, others, and the world. Understanding the long-term nature and quality of the client's relational connectedness is at the center of conducting a core issues assessment. This perspective presupposes that, given enough time, everyone will eventually experience some level of difficulty associated with relationship encounters. It is clear that some forms of abusive treatment can cause serious emotional and psychological harm, but many other less traumatic experiences can also create problems for an individual. Experiences such as loss, betrayal, abandonment, or being overprotected are just a few examples of relational encounters that can lead to maladaptive core issues. These types of experiences may occur for many different reasons throughout one's life. In some cases the hurts suffered in relationships have long-lasting effects and result in low self-esteem, repressed feelings, destructive patterns of behavior, difficulty in trusting others, and a whole host of unwanted feelings.

Even under the best of conditions, children will endure difficulties that are simply part of childhood. Two elements work in tandem to generate these difficulties. First, how is the child treated by others relative to having basic needs met? If the child is deprived of the emotional connection needed or is treated in a manner that is directly hurtful, such as in the case of physical abuse, relationally oriented difficulties may result. The second element that contributes to relationally oriented difficulties is the limited control children have over their environment (Parry & Doan, 1994). As a result, children must become adept at assessing their environments and develop strategies to adjust and adapt to that which they encounter in their young lives.

On one level, the struggles of childhood can be understood as instrumental to a child's psychosocial development. If it were not for various problematic situational conditions to which children must attend, it is unlikely that they would develop the broad array of socially oriented coping skills necessary for successful growth. In fact, many children are able to build strong skills sets in the relational arena and adjust well to the many perils of childhood. Although the skills that are developed as a result of rising to challenging situational conditions are clearly beneficial, this form of psychosocial learning can also result in an individual developing a problematic relational worldview that is consistent with one or more core issues.

A child who is fortunate enough to have been born into a family with loving and supportive parents still faces many difficult challenges. Conflicts with siblings, failure at school tasks, normal physical challenges, and negotiating peer group relationships all require varying degrees of emotion-focused coping. The situation is much worse for children who grow up in environments in which physical boundaries are violated, there is constant criticism, a lack of emotional caring, or any number of other extremely difficult relationally oriented events. Relational experiences that fail to meet important core emotional needs can evoke a variety of unwanted feelings. Difficult relational situations that do not respond to problem-focused coping efforts must be handled through a process of emotion-focused coping. The emotion-focused coping processes involved in managing those relational challenges serve to shape the nature of the core issues that develop and with which the individual may be forced to deal later in life. In this sense, core issues can be thought of as primary story themes that individuals act out in their day-to-day relationships with self, others, and the world. The degree of impairment with which the client struggles in acting out his or her core issue story is usually determined by the severity of the environment and the degree to which relational challenges are consistent over extended periods of time.

CONDUCTING THE ASSESSMENT

The core issues framework greatly aids in the assessment process because it helps the client give voice to the basic elements of the core problem. Assessing a client's core issues involves several tasks that draw on the clinician's ability to understand, analyze, synthesize, and evaluate many aspects of a client's life. Following a structured procedure is always helpful when tackling the complex task of assessment. This is especially true when conducting a core issues assessment because of the individual nature of core issues and the manner in which they are expressed in a client's life.

Four tasks are involved in completing a core issues assessment: (a) exploring the client's presenting problem, (b) generating hypotheses about the client's core issues, (c) tracing the client's psychosocial history to test the validity of core issues hypotheses, and (d) establishing a core issues conceptualization. Each task must be done carefully and completely to ensure an accurate assessment of the core issues and how they become active in the client's life.

Assessment Task I:
Exploring the Client's Presenting Problem

The initial phase in conducting a core issues assessment involves listening to the client's presenting problem and discerning the severity of the problems evident in the client's life. This phase of the assessment deviates little from the standard mental health intake format used in many counseling settings. The counselor should be active in obtaining information pertaining to the client's current level of functioning, the presence of any risk of harm, and the client's biological and psychosocial history. It is important to conduct a thorough assessment that meets the ethical and legal obligations of practice within the standard of care established by the profession (Corey, Corey, & Callanan, 2007; Madden, 1998). As previously stated, the core issues framework is a complementary adjunct to standard diagnostic procedures, not a replacement for those procedures. A standard intake interview form is provided in the Appendix at the end of this chapter.

During this first phase of core issues assessment, the counselor needs to pays special attention to the relational context within which the problem is being presented. In other words, which of the three types of relationships within the relational triad is the client identifying as being problematic? Is the client presenting a problem regarding relationship with self, relationship with another, or relationship with the nature of the world? Although the identified problem can shift over time as the client clarifies the nature of the core issues struggle, it is important to note at which point in the relational triad the client is most focused at the time of intake. Understanding the client's initial relational framing of the problem enables the counselor to more readily engage in empathic reflection, which enhances rapport building early in the counseling relationship. For example, a client displeased with one or more characteristics of self is focused on the "relationship with self" portion of the relational triad; this focus provides the counselor with a frame of reference for initial responses.

The counselor must also consider the presenting problem in the broader context of the client's life. During this step the counselor begins to think about differentiating the identified problem from the client's response to that problem. It is helpful during this assessment phase to remember that the problematic issues in an individual's life often reflect multiple interconnected problems; it is quite easy for the counselor to become confused by the many details a client may present. During the early phases of assessment, the counselor benefits from mentally organizing the information the client provides into two broad categories. Prompt the client to share why counseling is being requested. The client's initial response will either provide information about some sort of identified "problem" situation (for example, death of a loved one, loss of employment, a broken relationship, or marital conflict) or provide some form of "response to the problem" (for example, sad, hurt, angry, depressed, or anxious). It is important for the counselor to determine the degree to which the client understands the full scope of both the problem and how he or she is responding to that problem. Helping the client make this distinction is important in that many times what the client presents as the "problem" is just the first layer of a larger problematic picture. In addition, what the client presents as the problem might be more accurately described, from a more objective perspective, as a response to a more primary causal problem, or core issue. The case of Samantha illustrates this point.

The Case of Samantha

Samantha, age 34, reports to a counselor that she is in desperate need of help. She says that she has a drinking and drug problem. The counselor learns that 2 years ago Samantha was a successful pharmaceutical sales person making a very good living, but she lost her job due to drug and alcohol use. She reports that over the past 2 years she has been living off a substantial sum of money she had in a retirement fund account. During her initial interview, Samantha reports that she cannot believe how stupid she has been her whole life. As a result of her drug and alcohol use, she now has no job, no money, and is still using drugs and alcohol. Samantha reports that she is very frightened by the prospects of losing her house and that she feels intense anger in response to how she has allowed herself to get to this point.

It is clear that Samantha does have serious financial and substance use problems. There is certainly enough troubling evidence in her report to begin constructing interventions that relate directly to her substance use and financial difficulties, and certainly to assist her in developing a plan to find gainful employment. The counselor who is working from a core issues perspective, however, will also wonder if the set of problems Samantha has presented are part of a problematic pattern that has been generated in response to some other issue. Could there be a more basic issue or problem that can explain the difficulties with which Samantha now struggles? If so, the information Samantha has shared thus far is not "the problem" but rather her "response" to the problem.

By gathering information pertaining to her psychosocial history, the counselor discovers that along with feeling frightened and stupid, Samantha has experienced long-standing struggles with feelings of insecurity and feelings that she is unable to measure up to a rigid set of internalized standards. Despite many successes in school and in her early career, she reports feeling terrible about herself and lacks self-esteem. Samantha then tells the counselor that she began drinking in high school with friends and that doing so provided short-term relief from the negative feelings she had about herself. She began to use drugs in college to gain additional relief. At one point during the interview she stated, "No matter what I accomplished, I just did not feel like I was good enough. I felt like I could not measure up. I just felt so bad about myself. The alcohol and drugs helped to get rid of those feelings."

As a result of the counselor's probing, a larger problematic picture is revealed. Samantha's response to the problem was to use alcohol and take drugs as a means of dulling the negative feelings she held about herself. With this information the counselor is able to establish a number of important distinctions regarding Samantha's problem and her response to that problem. First, the relational context of Samantha's initial presenting problem is that she is angry with herself for creating the difficulties with which she now must deal, a problematic relationship with self. Second, the alcohol and drug use she reported as her problem is actually a response to a more basic problem of holding a negative view of herself and dealing with the feelings that come up as a result. Making these distinctions enables the counselor to focus the next step of the assessment more accurately and helps to ensure a clearer identification of Samantha's core issue.

Assessment Task II: Generating Initial Core Issues Hypotheses

Once the counselor has made an initial distinction between the client's problem and the client's response to that problem, the next question to address in the assessment is this: "What is the cause of the client's problem?" This is the key core issues question. To answer this question, the counselor conducts a thorough psychosocial history and compares that information with the thematic frames of core issue domains and individual core issues identified by Young (1999). This is a two-step process that involves first generating hypotheses of what the potential core issues for the client might be and then testing the validity of those hypotheses.

The Case of Samantha

In this phase of the assessment, the counselor engages in an active search for the cause of Samantha's problem by examining the core issues that continually generate negative feelings despite Samantha's many successes. By actively tracing Samantha's relational history and exploring the various points where Samantha may have engaged in emotion-focused coping, the counselor can pinpoint the cause of Samantha's problem. The counselor pays special attention to how Samantha's emotion-focused coping may have fostered the negative relationship she has established with herself. Specifically, the counselor attends to the nature of Samantha's past relational environments and the conditions she was exposed to over time that may be consistent with one or more core issues. A portion of an interview that demonstrates this aspect of history taking from a core issues perspective follows.

Counselor: Samantha, you say that you started to use alcohol in high school to feel better about yourself. Would you tell me more about that time of your life?

Samantha: There is not much to tell really. I was like everybody else in high school.

Counselor: Everybody else in high school. I am wondering what you mean when you say that.

Samantha: Well, you know. Kind of geeky, wanting to fit in and be liked, worried that you won't be liked, trying to do well with grades so you can get into a good college. Stuff like that.

Counselor: So you saw yourself, in your words, as geeky, wanting to have friends, and wanting to do well in school. Do I have that right?

Samantha: Yeah. That was pretty much it.

Counselor: So how did you make out in this area of your grades and having friends?

Samantha: Well, I did pretty well I guess. I mean my grades were pretty good.

Counselor: Pretty good? What does that mean?

Samantha: Well, I got very good grades by most people's standards. I was on the honor roll and received some academic scholarship money for college. A lot of money actually.

Counselor: That sounds very good. What about your friends?

Samantha: Oh, I had friends also. We used to talk on the phone a lot and hang out at each other's houses on weekends.

Counselor: So it sounds like you had a group you enjoyed.

Samantha: Yeah. I liked them a lot, but my parents thought they weren't good for me to hang with too much.

Counselor: Really, why was that?

Samantha: I don't know really. They just never seemed to approve of anything I did.

Counselor: I am not sure what you mean.

Samantha: My parents, well actually my mother, just had all of these rules and expectations of me. I could not just get good grades. I had to get the best grades. I had to have the right kind of friends. I couldn't laugh too loud. I had to wear the right clothes and always be conscious of how I looked. I had to be home earlier than all my other friends. Ya know, stuff like that. There were a lot of rules and expectations, and even though I would try to do my best to meet them, my mother was never happy. I would try and try, but she was never happy. She would say, "You could have done better" or "You could have done more." I could never please her. I could never measure up to her expectations.

Counselor: It sounds like that was tough for you.

Samantha: You don't even know how tough. All I ever wanted to do is measure up and meet her expectations but I never could. No matter what I did, no matter how hard I tried, no matter how successful I was, the only message I got was that I just never measured up.

In this snippet of the interview between Samantha and her counselor, we begin to get a sense of where problems exist in Samantha's relational world. She starts out with what sounds very much like a "relationship with self" problem, but the expectations her mother set for her as a child could be the source of a "relationship with other problem." This client's initial report needs additional probing and exploration. Samantha reported what is most immediately stressful or painful to her as the problem rather than acknowledging the core problem. The manner in which Samantha has responded to uncomfortable feelings of not measuring up to expectations appears to have created a second layer of employment and financial difficulties that must now also be addressed. The core issues perspective supports attending to Samantha's "response to problem" struggles along with the feelings she has tried to escape through substance use for the last 15 years. Although clearly problematic, the substance use in and of itself should not be framed as the problem or the core issue. Focusing on the drugs, alcohol, and employment without addressing Samantha's feelings about never being able to live up to a set of unrelenting standards she has internalized would greatly hamper work toward a positive outcome.

■

Assessment Task III:
Tracing the Client's Psychosocial History
to Test the Validity of Core Issues Hypotheses

A core issues assessment must be made cautiously. The counselor should never rush to judgment about the existence of any one particular core issue early in the assessment process. Rather, the counselor uses information collected in the interview first to build a preliminary core issue hypothesis and then to test the validity of that hypothesis, or lack thereof, with additional information. An intervention focused on the wrong core issue is less likely to be effective (Young et al., 2003). Particular elements in Samantha's presentation are significant from a core issues perspective, and these elements can be used to begin building a preliminary hypothesis about Samantha's story.

The Case of Samantha

First, there is some evidence, from Samantha's point of view, that her relational environment was harshly critical and restrictive. The core issues domain most closely associated with a restrictive relational environment is Overvigilance and Inhibition (Young, Weinberger, & Beck, 2001). Growing up in a relational environment that required Samantha to inhibit personal spontaneity restricted her expression of spontaneous feelings, impulses, and choices. As a result, Samantha became fearful or anxious if she acted on what she felt or wanted. Individuals who cope with an environment in which overvigilance and inhibition is an effective strategy are often so sensitive to what could go wrong, the mistakes they could make, or what might upset other people that they are very controlled and lack spontaneity.

The second key piece of information that emerges for Samantha's exchange with her counselor is that her mother imposed a rigid set of rules and expectations. These rules, as they have been presented thus far, seem to be a source for Samantha's feelings of never being able to "measure up" and her low self-esteem. Core issues in the domain of Overvigilance and Inhibition include "unrelenting standards." According to Young, Klosko, and Weishaar (2003), a client who has developed a core issue involving unrelenting standards tends to operate out of a sense that there is a right way to do everything. Everything should be done the proper and correct way without mistakes; one should strive to do things in a manner that ensures that nothing is incorrect. There is also a degree of rigidity about following rules. This core issue is expressed in a form of perfectionism in which there is an internalized belief that there is a right way and a wrong way to do things. These clients strive to meet internalized standards at the expense of their own gratification.

By matching the information from the client's reported psychosocial history against the structure of the various core issues templates, the counselor can begin to validate hypotheses regarding the types of core issues with which the client may be struggling. In Samantha's case there is initial evidence to support a hypothesis that at least one of the core issues with which she struggles is unrelenting standards. To form a full core issues conceptualization for Samantha, however, the counselor must also consider the expressed response to the core issue with which she struggles.

Assessment Task IV:
Assessing the Client's Response Style to the Core Issues

Once the counselor has conducted a full psychosocial assessment to validate initial hypotheses of a client core issue, the next task is to understand the client's specific responses and expressions of the core issue. One way to think about core issues is to conceptualize them as thematic presentations of the client's core issue story. The specific responses the client exhibits frame the manner in which the client lives out that core story. These specific responses illustrate the client's strategy for responding to the core issue when it is triggered.

Upon exposure to any situational condition, an individual will engage in a process of appraising the nature of the situational condition as well as the personal resources the individual has developed for dealing with the situation (see chapter 2). As a result of the appraisal process, the individual will engage in either problem-focused or emotion-focused coping (Lazarus, 1991). Within these two broad coping strategy categories there are individually specific coping styles.

A number of models have attempted to capture specific coping styles. Gladstone (1955) suggested seven styles of response options to a threatening stressor: counterthreat, attack, defend, compliance, defiance, avoidance, and circumvention. Carver, Scheier, and Weintraub (1989) proposed 15 individually specific coping behaviors: active coping, planning, suppression of competing activities, positive reinterpretation, restraint from action, seeking instrumental social support, seeking emotional social support, religion or spiritual support, humor, acceptance, focusing on and venting emotions, denial, mental disengagement, behavioral disengagement, and alcohol/drug use. Building on the work of Carver and colleagues, Zuckerman and Gagne (2003) specified five dimensions of coping based on analyzing the factor structure as well as convergent and discriminate validity studies of coping measures. These five dimensions are self-help, approach, accommodation, avoidance, and self-punishment.

Three basic themes would emerge in a content analysis of the coping dimensions across these three models: (a) a tendency to resist or fight against the threat, (b) a tendency to avoid the threat, or (c) a tendency to give in or surrender to the threat. Those familiar with adaptive reactions to stressful conditions may recognize the first two of these broad response styles as those popularized as the "fight or flight" response. That is, when confronted with a threatening situational condition, an individual's autonomic nervous system will physiologically prepare the individual either to stand and fight or to quickly move away from the threat. Seligman (1975) expanded on the idea of a fight or flight response when he advanced the concept known as "learned helplessness." If an animal is exposed to a painful shock and has no means of stopping or avoiding that stimulus, Seligman observed that the animal will surrender and endure the painful stimulus in a helpless manner. Seligman then generalized the concept of learned helplessness and surrender as a psychological dynamic applicable in a variety of human struggles.

Drawing on the stress and threat literature, Young, Klosko, and Weishaar (2003) suggested that three coping response styles can be expressed in response to a core issue threat. The threat, from a core issues perspective, is a relational condition that triggers some sense within the individual that a core emotional need will go unmet as it did during earlier formative periods of life (Young, 1999). When the core issue threat is triggered, the individual experiences a flood of intense thoughts and feelings and responds with one of three primary stylistic coping responses. Young labeled these coping response compensation adaptation, avoidance adaptation, and surrender adaptation.

Each of these responses to a stressful situational condition can be adaptive depending on the specific circumstances of the situation. For example,

Wrosch, Scheier, Carver, and Schulz (2003) advanced the idea that the action of goal disengagement, a form of avoidance response, can be adaptive in that it allows the individual to redirect energies in new directions that ultimately may serve the individual better over the longer term. Young et al. (2003) pointed out that when taken to an extreme any coping style becomes maladaptive. For example, an individual confronted with particular personal deficits might try to compensate for specific weaknesses by focusing more on strengths to counter those weaknesses. This coping response becomes maladaptive, however, when the person begins to overcompensate for a deficit by demanding personal perfection in everything and everyone. This type of overcompensation response is likely to create some form of difficulty for the individual over time. Maladaptive coping styles can become incorporated in the problematic core issue generated in response to situations that arise in the client's life.

To illustrate these coping response styles from a core issues perspective, let's briefly explore how Ayesha (see chapter 1), a 27-year-old woman dealing with the loss of yet another significant relationship, might employ each strategy. In her initial session Ayesha stated, "It is always the same old thing. I work so hard to make a relationship work, and in the end it is all for nothing."

In Ayesha's case, one key core issues assessment question is, "What motivates Ayesha to 'work so hard' to maintain her significant relationships?" As her history is traced, the counselor learns that Ayesha grew up in a family that can best characterized as having "an absence of loving presence." Her mother died when Ayesha was 8 years old, and her father, who was dedicated to providing for his children, worked for an engineering firm full time in addition to running his own consulting business. This combination of factors resulted in Ayesha often feeling alone and abandoned, first by her mother's death and later by her father not being present much of the day and evening due to work obligations.

The core issues domain that best characterizes Ayesha's relational family life is Disconnection and Rejection. Within this domain the core issue hypothesis that best captures Ayesha's core issue is abandonment/instability. This core issue is characterized by a relational worldview that people are not consistently reliable or are unavailable for support. Ayesha might exhibit any one of the three coping modalities in response to this abandonment core issue. She could try to compensate for her feelings of abandonment, try to avoid relationships to keep from feeling abandoned, or surrender to the feeling of abandonment.

Compensation Adaptation
When an individual overcompensates for a core issue, this coping response can result in a problematic pattern that interferes with goal attainment. Ayesha's coping response to abandonment was to overcompensate for the loss of her mother and the absence of her father by pursuing a strong love relationship. Her abandonment core issue predisposed her to experience a sense of abandonment whenever her partner was not readily present and engaged. Once triggered, Ayesha's abandonment core issue would mobilize a pattern of problematic relationally oriented behavior. Feeling that she might

be left alone again, she begins to express her neediness and wants reassurance of her partner's commitment. As her need escalates, Ayesha's partner experiences her as very needy, clingy, and emotionally smothering. As a result, her partner tends to emotionally distance himself, leaving Ayesha feeling abandoned yet again and longing for a close emotional connection even more. This cycle then repeats itself.

Avoidance Adaptation

Avoidance adaptation is characterized by cognitive, affective, or behavioral patterns that enable the individual to avoid a stressful situational condition. The individual's energies are mobilized to either minimize discomfort or avoid experiencing discomfort if at all possible. If Ayesha were to employ an avoidance adaptation to her abandonment core issue, she would be likely to close herself off from others and not allow herself to become emotionally close to anyone.

Surrender Adaptation

Surrender adaptation is characterized by the individual giving in to the core issue. The individual identifies with the characteristic elements of the core issue and accepts a role consistent with what the core issue expresses. Staying with the example of Ayesha's core issue of abandonment, a surrender adaptation might be expressed by Ayesha as not feeling deserving or worthy of having a close intimate connection with another person. She might say, "I am the person who others love to leave behind. I get very sad about it and even depressed, but that is who I am and that is all I can ever really expect."

Assessing the client's response style when a particular core issue is triggered helps the counselor develop a sense of the client's strategy for coping with the thoughts and feelings that any core issue generates. An assessment of client response style also serves to explain what motivates the client's response behaviors.

 The Case of Samantha

Now that the three basic coping responses have been illustrated, consider once again the case of Samantha. Recall that Samantha grew up in a home in which her mother imposed excessively rigid rules. As a result, Samantha often felt that she fell short of meeting parental expectations. Because of the standards set by her mother, Samantha lacked support for the core emotional need of spontaneity and play. Instead, successful achievement at very high standards was stressed on a consistent basis. This home environment is most consistent with the core issues domain Overvigilance and Inhibition. Samantha's life story is consistent with the core issue of unrelenting standards. Over time Samantha internalized those standards to a point that no matter what she was able to accomplish, she constantly felt like she "never measured up."

As stated earlier, understanding a client's individually specific coping responses helps the counselor understand the manner in which the client is acting out the core issue. For this reason, the counselor needs to note the client's coping response to the core issue threat. Samantha had three coping response options when her core issue of unrelenting standards was triggered. The first option is compensation adaptation; Samantha could work to overcome the feelings of "not measuring up" and continually strive to excel far beyond what is expected of her. Her second option is avoidance adaptation; she could remove herself from having to deal with the thoughts and feeling of not measuring up. The third option is surrender adaptation, giving in to the message that she has never measured up to her unrelenting standards and will never be able to do so. Under such a circumstance, it is not worth doing much of anything. Samantha stated that she used alcohol and drugs to escape from the feelings of never measuring up and low self-esteem. By framing of her drinking and drug use in this way, Samantha's coping strategy tends to be most closely associated with avoidance adaptation.

■

Assessment Task V:
Establishing a Full Core Issues Conceptualization

To this point in the assessment process, several different elements have been presented as specific aspects related to the process of conducting a core issues assessment. The counselor conducts an initial exploration of the client's presenting problem, generates an initial hypothesis about the client's core issue themes, and traces the client's psychosocial history to test the validity of the core issues hypotheses. The final step in the assessment process is to arrive at an overall conceptualization of the client and the nature of the client's current struggle. This last step involves pulling all of the elements of the assessment together to form a synthesized whole that expresses the nature of the core emotional need that went unmet, the specific core issue with which the client struggles, and the stylistic manner in which the core issue is expressed.

Establishing a full and accurate case conceptualization serves as the basis for establishing short- and long-term outcome goals and guides implementation of the counseling plan and associated interventions. Figure 3.1 illustrates the coping style and relational orientation assessment model. The dimensions used to describe the client are coping style and relational focus, and each dimension has three elements. Coping style describes the nature of the client's response to the problem. The relational focus addresses with whom,

FIGURE 3.1

The Coping Style and Relational Orientation Assessment Model

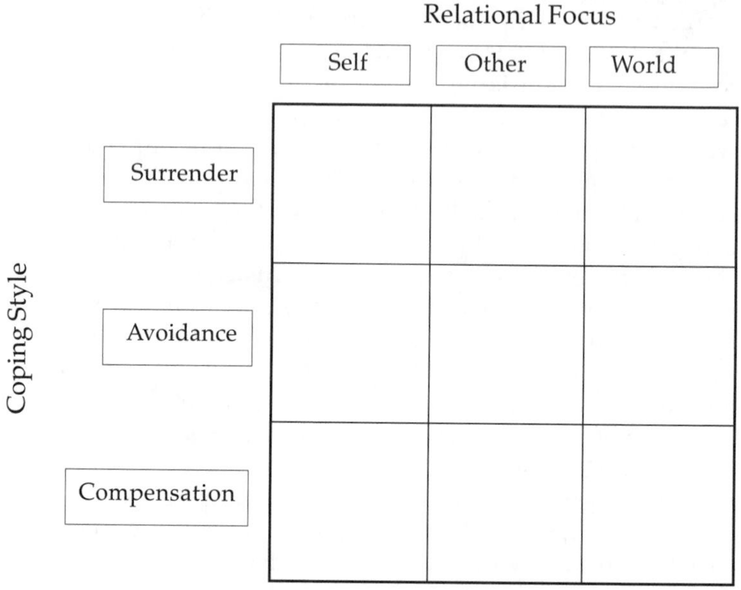

Relational Focus

	Self	Other	World
Surrender			
Avoidance			
Compensation			

Coping Style

or with what, the problematic core issue is relationally associated in the client's life. This model presupposes that the three elements across the two dimensions are always present, function in combination with one another, and can usually be identified and described.

A framework to help with the basic identification of coping adaptation for each of the client core issues is presented in Table 3.1. It is important to filter the content of the client's story through these coping processes so that the nature of the relational struggle with the self, others, or the world can be adequately addressed.

The Case of Samantha

At this point in conducting an assessment of Samantha's struggle, the counselor should be able to provide a full clinical description. Along with the psychiatric diagnosis of substance abuse, the counselor can state with a degree of certainty that spontaneity and play was a core emotional need that was difficult to meet and, based on her reported history, Samantha struggles with the core issue of unrelenting standards. Further, as depicted in Figure 3.2, Samantha has internalized the core issue of unrelenting standards, and as a result, the relational focus of her presented problem is with herself. When her core issue is triggered and evokes negative thoughts and

TABLE 3.1

Examples of Maladaptive Coping Responses

Early Maladaptive Schema	Examples of Surrender	Examples of Avoidance	Examples of Compensation
Abandonment/ Instability	Selects partner who cannot make commitment and remains in the relationship	Avoids intimate relationships; drinks a lot when alone	Clings to and "smothers" the partner away; vehemently attacks partner for even minor separation
Mistrust/Abuse	Selects abusive partner and permits abuse	Avoids becoming vulnerable and trusting anyone; keeps secrets	Uses and abuses others ("get others before they get you")
Emotional Deprivation	Selects emotionally depriving partner and does not ask partner to meet needs	Avoids intimate relationships altogether	Acts emotionally demanding with partner and close friends
Defectiveness/ Shame	Selects critical and rejecting friends; puts self down	Avoids expressing true thoughts and feelings and does not let others get close	Criticizes and rejects others while seeming to be perfect
Social Isolation/ Alienation	At social gatherings, focuses exclusively on differences from others rather than similarities	Avoids social situations and groups	Becomes a chameleon to fit into groups
Dependence/ Incompetence	Asks significant others (parents, spouse) to make all his or her financial decisions	Avoids taking on new challenges, such as learning to drive	Becomes so self-reliant that he or she does not ask anyone for anything ("counterdependent")
Vulnerability to Harm or Illness	Obsessively reads about catastrophes in newspapers and anticipates them in everyday situations	Avoids going places that do not seem totally "safe"	Acts recklessly, without regard to danger ("counter-phobic")
Enmeshment/ Undeveloped Self	Tells mother everything, even as an adult; lives through partner	Avoids intimacy; stays independent	Tries to become the opposite of significant others in all ways
Failure	Does tasks in a halfhearted or haphazard manner	Avoids work challenges completely; procrastinates on tasks	Becomes an "overachiever" by ceaselessly driving him- or herself
Entitlement/ Grandiosity	Bullies others into getting own way, brags about own accomplishments	Avoids situations in which he or she is average, not superior	Attends excessively to the needs of others
Insufficient Self-Control/ Self-Discipline	Gives up easily on routine tasks	Avoids employment or accepting responsibility	Becomes overly self-controlled or self-disciplined
Subjugation	Lets other individuals control situations and make choices	Avoids situations that might involve conflict with another individual	Rebels against authority

(Continued on next page)

TABLE 3.1

Examples of Maladaptive Coping Responses

Early Maladaptive Schema	Examples of Surrender	Examples of Avoidance	Examples of Compensation
Self-Sacrifice	Gives a lot to others and asks for nothing in return	Avoids situations involving giving or taking	Gives as little as possible
Approval-Seeking/ Recognition-Seeking	Acts to impress others	Avoids interacting with those whose approval is coveted	Goes out of the way to provoke the disapproval of others; stays in the background
Negativity/ Pessimism	Focuses on the negative; ignores the positive; worries constantly; goes to great lengths to avoid any possible negative outcome	Drinks to blot out pessimistic feelings and unhappiness	Is overly optimistic ("Pollyanna"-ish); denies unpleasant realities
Emotional Inhibition	Maintains a calm, emotionally flat demeanor	Avoids situations in which people discuss or express feelings	Awkwardly tries to be the "life of the party," even though it feels forced and unnatural
Unrelenting Standards/ Hypercriticalness	Spends inordinate amounts of time trying to be perfect	Avoids situations or procrastinates over tasks in which performance will be judged	Does not care about standards at all; does tasks in a hasty, careless manner
Punitiveness	Treats self and others in harsh, punitive manner	Avoids others for fear of punishment	Behaves in overly forgiving way

Note. From *Schema therapy: A practitioner's guide* (pp. 38–39), by J. E. Young, J. S. Klosko, and M. Weishaar, 2003, New York: Guilford Press. Reprinted with permission.

feelings, Samantha employs an avoidance coping adaptation by ingesting drugs and alcohol. With a full descriptive conceptualization in place, the counselor is better able to design an intervention that not only incorporates Samantha's drug and alcohol use but also address the core elements that are central to Samantha's problem and motivates her substance use behavior.

■

SUMMARY

This chapter presented an assessment process that was carried out by performing five different but related tasks. The first task is to conduct an initial exploration of the client's presenting problem. This initial exploration deviates little from what counselors do in many counseling settings that use a

FIGURE 3.2

Samantha's Avoidance of Self Problematic Orientation

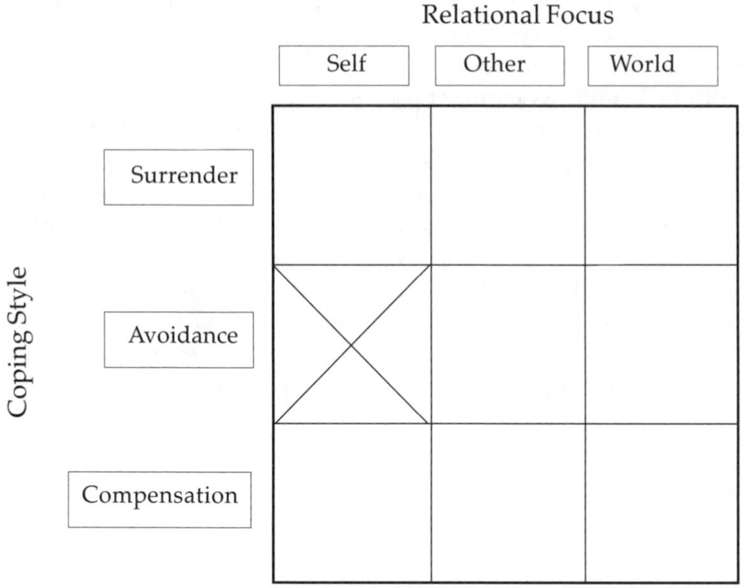

Relational Focus

	Self	Other	World

Coping Style:
- Surrender
- Avoidance
- Compensation

standard mental health intake format. The counselor's goal is to obtain information pertaining to the client's current level of functioning, the presence of any risk of harm, and the client's biological and psychosocial history. The counselor should also work to make an initial distinction between the client's problem and the client's response to that problem.

The second task in the assessment process is to generate initial core issue hypotheses. Once the counselor has made an initial distinction between the problem and the client's response to that problem, the focus shifts toward determining the core issue source of the client's problem. The core issues are identified by comparing the client's psychosocial history with information in the thematic frames of core issue domains and individual core issue elements. The process of comparing the client's psychosocial history with any core issue profile is a gradual one and involves first generating hypotheses of what the potential core issues for the client might be and then testing the validity of those hypotheses.

The third task in the assessment process is to trace the client's psychosocial history to test the validity of the core issues hypotheses. A core issues assessment must be made cautiously; the counselor should never rush to judgment about the existence of any one particular core issue. Rather, the counselor must use information collected in the interview to first build a preliminary core issue hypothesis and then to work toward testing the validity of that hypothesis using additional historic information. An intervention focused on the wrong core issue is likely to generate an ineffective counseling intervention.

The fourth task in the assessment process is to assess the client's response or coping style when a particular core issue is triggered. This fourth task involves working toward an understanding of the client's individually specific responses and expressions of the core issue. Three different responses or adaptations to core issues were identified: compensation adaptations, avoidance adaptations, and surrender adaptations.

The fifth task in the assessment process is to synthesize the information that has been collected and articulate the nature of the core emotional need that went unmet, the specific core issue with which the client struggles, and the stylistic manner in which the core issue is expressed. The client's coping style describes the nature of the client's response to the problem. The relational focus addresses with whom, or with what, the problematic core issue is relationally associated. Once this final step in the assessment process is completed, the counselor can design an intervention that not only incorporates the client's initial problematic concern but also addresses the core elements central to generating the problem and motivating behavior.

APPENDIX

Counseling Intake Assessment Form

Date: _____ Work Phone: _____

Client Name: _____ Home Phone: _____

Address: _____

_____

Gender: _____ Age: _____

Ethnicity and Race: _____ Socioeconomic Status: _____

PRESENTING PROBLEM(S):

Duration of the presenting problem:

History of presenting problem and/or similar problems in the past:

RISK ASSESSMENT:

Current or past ideation of harmful behaviors (Suicide and Homicide):

Intention to take action on thoughts of harming self or others:

Specificity of plan(s):

Availability of means:

Lethality of method:

History of harmful behaviors (self, relatives, friends):

CLIENT HISTORY:

History of Interpersonal Relationships:
(include quality of peer relationships, significant losses, separations)

Academic History:
(include any remarkable indicators such as being developmentally gifted, or delayed, or having learning disabilities)

Work History:

History of Legal Problems and/or Destructive Behaviors:

Alcohol/Drug History and Current Use Behaviors:

History of Self-Abusive Behaviors:
(for example, eating, sex, laxatives, spending, cutting oneself)

History of Sexual Abuse:
(for example, past or present, nature and duration, abuse of other family members, any warning signs or indicators of abuse in current relationship)

History of Previous Counseling:
_____ Yes _____ No

If yes, when, with whom (name and phone number of past counselors), what issues were addressed, and will client give you a release to contact the former counselor?

List psychiatric medications and dosage presently or in the past:

HEALTH STATUS:
(Any history of health problems)
Date of last physical exam:

History and/or Current Status of any Health Conditions:

Medications:
_____ No _____ Yes
Name(s) of Medication(s)   Dose

Level of regular physical activity:
_____ High _____ Moderate _____ Low _____ None
Type(s) of physical activity:

SPIRITUALITY:
(Religious affiliation or other spiritual practice)
Role that spirituality plays in client's life:

Reported level of satisfaction with spiritual endeavor:

MENTAL STATUS ASSESSMENT:
I. Social Presentation
  Appearance:
  Grooming:

_____Normal _____Disheveled _____Unusual *(explain):*

  Hygiene:

_____Normal _____Body Odor _____Bad Breath _____Other *(explain):*

Interpersonal Style:

_____ Separates Comfortably From Parents *(Child)*	_____ Manipulative
_____ Separates Too Easily From Parents *(Child)*	_____ Impulsive
	_____ Fearful
_____ Would Not Separate at All *(Child)*	_____ Apathetic/Withdrawn
_____ Appropriate, Cooperative	_____ Silly
_____ Domineering, Demanding	_____ Destructive
_____ Provocative	_____ Dependent
_____ Guarded	_____ Crying
_____ Submissive, Passive	_____ Preoccupied
_____ Threatening, Hostile, Aggressive	_____ Ambivalent
	_____ Competitive
_____ Pouty	_____ Self-Destructive
	_____ Other *(explain)*:

Eye Contact:

_____ Unremarkable	
_____ Maintains Good Eye Contact	_____ Stares Into Space
_____ Avoids Eye Contact	_____ Other *(explain)*:

Speech:

_____ Normal	_____ Monotone
_____ Pressured	_____ Rambling
_____ Slow	_____ Mute
_____ Whiny	_____ Impaired
_____ Overly Loud	_____ Broken
_____ Stutters	_____ Incoherent
_____ Babyish	_____ Other *(explain)*:

II. Behavioral/Affective/Psychomotor Functioning

Motor Activity:

_____ Appropriate	_____ Hyperactive
_____ Relaxed	_____ Mannerisms
_____ Slow, Underactive	_____ Tremors
_____ Sedate	_____ Tics
_____ Psychomotor Retardation	_____ Poor Coordination
_____ Restless	_____ Other *(explain)*:
_____ Pacing	

Impulse Control:

_____ Good

_____ Fair

_____ Poor

Mood:

_____ Normal/Appropriate	_____ Depressed
_____ Elated	_____ Anxious
_____ Optimistic, Cheerful	_____ Angry
_____ Pessimistic	_____ Suspicious
_____ Guilty	_____ Other *(explain)*:

Affect:

_____ Appropriate   _____ Labile
_____ Inappropriate   _____ Constricted
_____ Blunted, Flat   _____ Other *(explain)*:

III. Cognitive Processes

Orientation:

_____ × 3 (person, place, self)
_____ Disoriented
_____ Other *(explain)*:

Attention:

_____ Normal
_____ Distractible
_____ Hypervigilant

Perception:

_____ Normal   _____ Visual Hallucinations
_____ Auditory Hallucinations   _____ Other *(explain)*:

Insight:

_____ Fair to Good   _____ Absent; Denies Problems
_____ Limited *(difficulty*   _____ Blames Others for Problems
        acknowledging   _____ Other *(explain)*:
        problems)

Memory:

_____ Intact   _____ Impaired Recent
_____ Impaired Immediate Recall   *(2 hours to 4 days)*
        (10 to 30 sec)   _____ Impaired Recent Past
_____ Impaired Short-Term   *(past few months)*
        (up to 1½ hours)   _____ Impaired Remote Past
     (6 months to lifetime)

Thought Processes / Content:

_____ Unremarkable   _____ Confused
_____ Flight of Ideas   _____ Tangential, Circumstantial
_____ Blocking   _____ Obsessive
_____ Loose Associations   _____ Delusions
_____ Confabulation   _____ Suicidal
_____ Incoherent

Ideation:

_____ Homicidal Ideation   _____ Ideas of Reference
_____ Magical Thinking   _____ Other *(explain)*:

Judgment:

_____ Good   _____ Poor; Limited
_____ Fair to Good   _____ Significantly Impaired

IV. Intellectual Ability

Overall Intellectual Level:

_____ Below Average   _____ Superior
_____ Average   _____ Cannot Determine
_____ Above Average   _____ Other *(explain)*:

_____ General Information
 (*Past four presidents, governor of the state, state capital, direction of sunrise and sunset, and so forth*)
_____ Calculations
 (*Serially subtracting 7 from 100. Simple multiplication word problems such as, "If a pencil costs 5 cents, how many pencils can you buy with 45 cents?"*)
_____ Abstract Reasoning
 (*Explanation of proverbs. This assesses the ability to make valid generalizations. Responses may be literal, concrete, personalized, or bizarre. Example proverbs: "Still waters run deep," or "A rolling stone gathers no moss."*)
_____ Opposites
 (*Fast/Slow, Big/Small, Hard/Soft*)
_____ Similarities
 (*Door/Window, Telephone/Radio, Dog/Cat, Apple/Banana*)
_____ Attention
 (*Digit Span, or Trials to Learn Four Words*)
_____ Concentration
 (*Months of the Year or Days of the Week Backwards*)
_____ Reasoning and Judgment
 (*The client is able to connect consequences to choices and behavior.*)

FAMILY HISTORY:
(*Construct and attach genogram if appropriate*)

DSM-IV MULTIAXIAL DIAGNOSIS

	Diagnosis	*Code Number*	*Diagnosis*	*Code Number*
Axis I				
Axis II				
Axis III				
Axis IV				

Axis V Current: _____ Highest in Last Year:_____

COUNSELOR'S CONCEPTUALIZATION OF THE CLIENT:

COUNSELOR AND CLIENT GOALS FOR COUNSELING:

INITIAL COUNSELING PLAN:
(*Use additional sheets as necessary*)

CHAPTER 4

Designing the Counseling Intervention: Framing the Client's Living Story

■

Once the assessment is complete, the next step is to construct and implement a counseling intervention plan. It is not possible to address all of the counseling orientations and intervention modalities a counselor may chose from. Instead, this chapter provides an overview of one approach that is consistent with the conceptualization of the core issues framework described in previous chapters.

■

CLIENT CORE ISSUES EXPRESSED AS A LIVING STORY

An effective counseling plan addresses the client's problem in a manner conceptually consistent with how that problem exists within the context of the client's life. In other words, the work in which the counselor and client engage should be consistent with the overall understanding of the problem and the mutually agreed upon goal of counseling (Horvath & Greenberg, 1987).

Consider for a moment the nature of a core issues conceptualization. In chapter 2 a core issue was defined as the primary problematic elements of one's intrapersonal and interpersonal meaning-making system that, when activated, serve to generate problematic responses to specific situational conditions. When an individual is experiencing problems in life, there is consistency in the manner in which that individual responds to those problems. Therefore, a client's problem can be examined within a context of broader thematic expressions of one or more core issues. Furthermore, these themes tend to emerge when the client is confronted with specific trigger situations. Because these response themes reflect the dynamic elements of a client's core issues, they can also serve as a frame for understanding a particular type of living story about the problematic nature of a client's life struggles. An example will illustrate this point.

Consider once again the case of Bill, an 18-year-old college freshman who was feeling inadequate to manage living independently from his family (see chapter 1). Bill's response to this problem included feelings of fear, constant anxiety, sleep disturbance, intrusive thoughts of failing, and worry that he is "going crazy." Forming a working diagnosis for this client is, in one sense, pretty straightforward. Given the limited amount of information presented, a counselor might think in terms of one or more Axis I disorders, such as adjustment disorder, major depressive episode anxious type, or separation anxiety. Understanding this client's core issue rests not within the detail of presented symptoms but within the context of a living story that speaks to how the client is making meaning about his current situation, how the client responds to core issue triggers, and what aspects of his history have brought him to feeling so vulnerable at this point in his life. Again, what the client reports as the problem and the manner in which a client responds to the problem is of paramount importance. It is important to remember that the client's response to the problem can be as problematic as the problem itself, and in some cases the response to the problem can be even more problematic. The counselor must form a clear understanding about what the client defines as the problem and what can be directly observed or indirectly inferred as the client's response to the problem.

In most cases, differentiating what the client reports as the problem and the client's response to the problem is relatively easy. Clients are generally quite good at reporting the difficult situations or uncomfortable feelings that have motivated them to seek counseling. The client's response to the problem is, in most cases, also easily accessed. A client will usually offer this information directly to the counselor. Alternatively, by using basic listening skills, the counselor can help the client clarify the specific manner in which he or she attempted to deal with the problem. As has been detailed in earlier chapters, however, assessing client core issues is a bit of a departure from the assessment process used to arrive at a traditional DSM-IV-TR five-axis diagnosis. A core issues assessment provides the structure necessary for discovering what underlies the client's problem and generates the client's living story of intrapersonal or interpersonal struggle.

CONSTRUCTIVISTS, LIVING STORIES, AND CORE ISSUES

An individual's living story consists of the repetitive reenactments of his or her personal truth expressed through relational interactions over time. The living story reflects the client's relational worldview of self, others, and the nature of the outside world. The living story is an expression of the client's personal relational orientation and explains how the client goes about attempting to satisfy perceived needs and wishes. The client's story can provide the counselor with some idea of how the client contextualizes his or her relational world and responds to it.

Individuals are not born with a personal living story. Living stories are constructed through a process of interaction with self, or others, and the world. According to Kegan (1982), we are constantly engaged in a process of making observations of the world and then cognitively constructing an organized, meaningful whole from those observations. This act of making meaning is a primary hallmark of what it means to be human. Perry (1970) conveyed this concept most elegantly when he suggested that "What organisms do is organize and what human organisms do is organize meaning" (p. 3).

From a postmodern constructivist perspective, the act of observing, assessing, and organizing meaning results in the formation of a particular version of reality. One can think of a personally constructed reality as a personal "truth" that serves as a foundation for how an individual perceives and responds to the environment (Babrow, Kline, & Rawlins, 2005; Parry & Doan, 1994; Ramsay, 1998). Constructivists contend that there are limits to any form of objective knowing (or truth) derived from one's meaning-making process (Spence, 2003). Individually constructed worldviews sometimes support thoughts, feelings, and behaviors that are problematic in nature. In other words, if an individual is encapsulated in a set of maladaptive truths, the actions that are generated from those truths will result in life experiences that may be incongruent with desired goals and outcomes.

The idea that individuals engage in a process of constructing personal truths in their lives provides the counselor with both a challenging obstacle and a fortunate advantage. From a counseling perspective, the challenge is that these personal truths are not easily relinquished. The intrapersonal and interpersonal consequences of thoughts, feelings, and behaviors, informed by core issue truths, form the historical context for how the client functions in life. Because personally constructed truths, by their nature, reflect an encapsulated reality, there is often very little awareness of alternative pathways, and the problematic issues in a client's life remain amazingly consistent and repetitive. The self seeks to maintain a high degree of homeostatic consistency, so problematic patterns are relatively stable. In this regard the self has inherent integrity that is resistant to change. The counselor is in a position to observe the client's special kind of loyalty to repetitively patterns of behavior that result in undesirable outcomes. This characteristic of the self poses a very interesting set of challenges when designing a counseling plan aimed at changing undesirable behavior patterns.

On the other hand, the idea of subjectively constructed truths carries with it a fortunate advantage. This advantage is embedded in this idea that if "truth" is not objective but rather a personally subjective construction, then that "truth" can be deconstructed, each part examined objectively, and then reconstructed in a manner more adaptive and supportive of a client's life needs and desires. If the counselor can engage the client in a process of softening a constructed truth that is maladaptive, other more adaptive perspectives can be taken in by the client for consideration. Specific personal truths can be transformed, and together counselor and client can work to create a truth that is more goal congruent (Parry & Doan, 1994).

Core Issues and the Living Story Narratives

In narrative approaches, the counselor examines various elements of a client's story to understand the nature of the problems presented and to design appropriate counseling interventions. Each person has stories that reflect important events that have left a lasting impression and have served to help that person establish truths about the self, what to expect from others, and the nature of the world. These stories capture the essence of the forces that have shaped an individual's life in profound ways. The themes of these stories can be understood as the expressions of individual, social, and cultural contexts through which the client establishes meaning in life. Certain stories express the core problematic issues with which the client may struggle over time. This idea was captured extremely well by Polkinghorne (1988):

> Narrative is a scheme by means of which human beings give meaning to their experience of temporality and personal actions. Narrative meaning functions to give form to the understanding of a purpose to life and to join everyday actions and events into episodic units. It provides a framework for understanding the past events of one's life and for planning future actions. It is the primary scheme by means of which human existence is rendered meaningful. (p. 11)

Consciously experiencing the expression of one's own personal narrative can bring to the personal center the painful aspects of life with which a person attempts to cope.

Counselors can look beyond the problem statements and symptoms that a client may present and begin to hear the essence of who this person is in the context of the client's core issue story. Hearing the client's whole story and listening for the key elements that signify the client's core struggle is no easy task (Parry & Doan, 1994; Spence, 2003). As Wanner (1994) states, "Another problem with understanding the nature of narrative lies is the fact that it comes in so many guises" (p. 17). Although helping clients to understand their narratives may be difficult, it is important nonetheless. Lane (1993) suggested that one of the most important aspects of working with survivors of traumatic experiences is to help them focus inward, remember the events that serve as personal historic mile markers, and reflect on the meaning that these events hold. By engaging in this process, individuals learn more about who they are within a framework of their own history. The personal "living" story offers the client a unique opportunity to gain an understanding of the three types of human relationships (self, others, and the nature of the world). By focusing on the narrative underlying the core stories of the client's life, the counselor can help the client gain an awareness that might otherwise go unacknowledged. Wanner (1994) suggested that the goal of the helping professional is to assist the client in telling his or her story so that a sense of unity and wholeness is created within the self.

Client Narratives and Culture

Culture establishes the foundation for many meaning-making processes: It defines the nature of one's personal worldview and therefore structures the individual's understanding of self, others, and the world. The broad, overlapping nature of cultural influence on an individual's life includes family heritage, gender, community, religion, sexual orientation, level of socioeconomic advantage, physical ability, ethnicity, race, and geographic region. Counselors must be cognizant of the role that multiple cultures may play in shaping a client's worldview. These overlapping cultural influences establish a context for constructing specific meaning-making processes that are expressed as personal narratives (Halliday, 1989; Hardy, 1977; Howard, 1989; McHale, 1992; Nussbaum, 1988; Polkinghorne, 1988; Wanner, 1994; Witherell & Noddings, 1991). Perhaps Bruner (1990) captured this idea best when he wrote the following about how culture is reflected in narrative:

> It deals . . . with the stuff of human action and human intentionality. It mediates between the canonical world of culture and the more idiosyncratic world of beliefs, desires, and hopes. It renders the exceptional comprehensible and keeps the uncanny at bay . . . it reiterates the norms of society without being didactic. And . . . it provides a basis for rhetoric without confrontation. It can even teach, conserve memory, or alter the past. (p. 52)

Many of the early inputs to the construction of the client's living story are determined by the nature of family culture and the general state of affairs of the environment. Two factors are important here. First, regardless of how wonderful or wretched one's childhood is, the primary task of early life is to survive in a world where one has very little power. This early life situation results in the construction of a childhood survival story. The second factor is the fact that young children are unable to cognitively engage in anything other than dualistic thinking. The survival story is constructed from limited personal experience and a narrow perspective. It is, however, known to be "the truth." These early survival stories form the basis for the client's reality and are rarely questioned. This reality becomes an ingrained story of the individual's relational life. Parry and Doan (1994) captured the essence of this phenomenon:

> If the stories into which children are born, create and shape their emotions, they do so by constructing what the children *believe* to be real. . . . The more, however, their very survival seems to be threatened . . . the more rigidly incorporated such stories become. When a child's world-shaping stories come to imply risks to his/her survival, they include two significant messages: "This is what you must avoid to survive" (either physically or psychologically) and "This is what you can do to survive"—and maybe even be loved. (p. 38)

It is important to keep in mind that children have no choice but to operate from a set of basic core emotional needs. As each of those needs expands through the stages of development, it is reasonable to conceptualize each of the needs as contributing an element to a child's living story. The story starts with children wanting and needing most to know—as a matter of survival—that they will be cared for. With this very basic need as a foundation for the living story, the core of the living story can be accessed by determining the conditions necessary for the child to feel loved and protected. Parry and Doan (1994) suggested that the normal socialization process uses the need for love and caring by setting conditions for the child in the form of an "if-then" statement: "If only you will do _____, then I [we] will love you." Children readily fall prey to this if-then message because they have little power over what happens in their environment and at the same time need to feel loved and secure.

Each of the five core issue domains identified by Young and colleagues (2003) relates to specific core emotional needs that were not adequately met. The unmet core needs are the basis for developing an understanding of the core issue narrative or the client's problematic living story. Within these five domains are 18 core issues, each with three different coping adaptations (see Table 3.1). It follows that there are 18 basic core issue narratives, each with three variations based on whether the client employs a compensation, avoidance, or surrender coping adaptation. An example will illustrate how the counselor can work within this core issues framework to establish the problematic theme of the client's narrative.

The Case of Kara

Kara is a 21 year-old senior in college. Prior to going away to school, she lived with her mother and 19-year-old brother. As young children, Kara and her brother had separate special relationships with the opposite gender parent. Kara was her father's favorite, and her brother was her mother's favorite. She was just 8 years old when her father was diagnosed with a rare form of bone cancer. The only hope for her father's survival was an experimental bone marrow transplant procedure that required a long period of hospitalization. Because the treatment greatly compromised his immune system, Kara was not allowed to visit her father. Instead she was told that her father would be home soon and that she would be able to spend time with him then. Despite a long course of medical treatment, Kara's father died at the hospital without her ever seeing him again. To make matters worse, Kara's mother was deeply depressed for years following the death of her husband. These depressive episodes often lasted for months at a time. During each of her mother's depressive episodes, Kara was sent to live with her aunt, a single working woman who took very little interest in her. Kara often felt alone, left behind, and unloved.

After hearing Kara's story, the counselor made some preliminary hypotheses regarding the core issues that might be at work in Kara's life. The loss of her father and the emotional absence of her mother during childhood led the counselor, at least initially, to the core issue domain of Disconnection and Rejection and, within that domain, to the possible core issues of abandonment/instability and emotional deprivation–nurturance type.

The next step is to determine how Kara responds when one of these core issues is triggered. Determining how and when Kara's core issue is triggered aids greatly in understanding the nature of her story. In this case example, only the core issue of abandonment/instability will be addressed.

Depending on which of the three coping responses Kara employs to deal with her core issue of abandonment/instability, the counselor could see one of three different narrative themes. If Kara responds to the core issue with a compensation coping adaptation, she might express an intense level of neediness and constantly attempt to form very close relationships with others. If Kara employs an avoidance coping adaptation strategy, she might demonstrate a complete lack of interest in forming any close relationships so as not to set herself up for being abandoned again. If she employs a surrender coping adaptation style, Kara might seek relationships with those who are most likely to be emotionally distant or dismissive of her in general, resulting in repeated episodes to experience abandonment.

▪

Once the client's core issue has been identified, the counselor conducts an analysis of the client's coping adaptation response to clarify an important and dynamic element in the client's story. Understanding the client's specific coping adaptation enables the counselor to determine what is motivating the client's response to a perceived problem. This understanding helps the counselor empathize more fully with the client's relational worldview.

The Temporal Elements and Core Issue Stories

The final step in addressing the client's core issue narrative is to listen for the degree of consistency in the various stories that the client relates across time. There are three possibilities when considering the temporal elements of client stories. The stories will either have taken place in the past, are taking place in the present, or are anticipated to take place in the future (Ricoeur, 1984). Stories from the past provide the counselor with a view of the client's personal history. Stories about the present provide a frame for understanding the client's present situational struggle. Stories about the future connote either hopes or fears that the client is holding. A client's narrative can be constructed from this temporal triad in light of the three possible coping adaptations and the three self-in-relationship options. Figure 4.1 provides a graphic representation of this model for analyzing a living story. Having

FIGURE 4.1

Model for Analyzing the Living Story

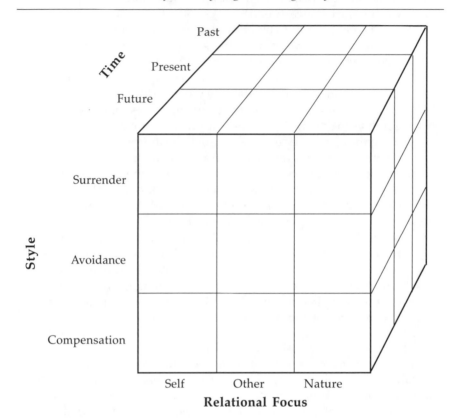

such a model can increase the ease in synthesizing the core issue narrative from a confluence of stories the client conveys about self, others, or the world across a personal time line.

DESIGNING AND IMPLEMENTING THE COUNSELING INTERVENTION

Once the counselor has assessed the nature of the core issue struggles and the nature of that client's living story narrative, a counseling intervention can be designed and implemented. Again, this chapter is not intended as a comprehensive counseling methods primer for all possible interventions available to counselors. However, counselors using a variety of methods may find this perspective a useful adjunct to their repertoire.

It is hoped that you now have a clear understanding of the thesis that has been presented thus far. This thesis holds that an individual lives by the subjective truths that are constructed about his or her relationship with self, others, and the nature of the world. These constructed truths are reflected in a number of living stories, which form an individual's personal narrative and manifest as expressions of that individual's relational reality. Individuals begin constructing their set of personal truths during childhood, usually in an environment over which the child has little control. These "truths" help the child cope with and manage difficult childhood challenges. When the environment is abnormally protective, inconsistent and chaotic, abusive, rigid, or in some way threatening, the personal truths established will reflect the environment within which the child must attempt to survive and adapt. As the child becomes an adolescent and later an adult, these childhood stories can become outdated and may no longer be useful as the person's living environment changes. As a result, these old stories can become the source of problems rather than being the adaptive coping solutions they once were.

Using the client core issues framework, the goal of any counseling intervention is to address the client's subjectively constructed truths about self, others, and the world. The counselor works toward four process goals when designing and implementing a counseling intervention based on a client's core issues living story. The first goal is to help the client clearly understand and articulate the nature of the core issues that are operating in that individual's life. The second goal is to help the client understand how those particular core issues have been the source for the client's problems and serve to perpetuate a problematic living story. The first two goals are accomplished by conducting the core issues assessment and helping the client connect the nature of these core issues to the client's current struggles. The third goal is to help the client deconstruct various elements of the core issues story and question the subjective truths upon which that story has been constructed. Once the counselor and client have deconstructed the living story, the fourth broad goal is to help the client reconstruct a more adaptive story that reflects the outcomes the client desires.

During this process, the client shifts away from the history entrenched survival story constructed in childhood and toward a new story that is self-authored and congruent with the client's current needs and desires (Parry & Doan, 1994). Ideally the counselor will help the client create a relational worldview toward self, others, and the nature of the world that allows for more adaptive thoughts, feelings, and behavioral responses to that which has been defined as the problem. Goals three and four encompass the bulk of counseling sessions, and for this reason they will be addressed in detail in the following section.

DECONSTRUCTING AND RECONSTRUCTING THE CLIENT'S LIVING STORY

According to Parry and Doan (1994), the process of story deconstruction and reconstruction consists of a series of elements that help the client to become more adaptive in life. These elements comprise a set of tasks that counselor and client work through over the course of the counseling process: (1) identify the childhood survival story; (2) support the client for doing what needed to be done to survive; (3) connect the common elements of the various core issues stories and clarify the assumptive truths that have been constructed about the self, others, and the nature of the world; (4) examine the story as being external to the self; (5) identify the core issue trigger points and how those issues, when activated, generate strong feelings, thoughts, and behaviors; (6) identify the limitations of this old, less adaptive story; (7) help the client establish the ways and means to stop responding to the old story; and (8) help the client create a new alternative story. Counselor and client work methodically through each step in this process.

Task 1: Identification of the Survival Story

During childhood the individual begins to construct subjective truths about self, others, and the nature of the world. The child is constantly assessing the environment and drawing meaning from his or her experience. At the most basic level, the child is deciding how to best interact with the environment as a means for survival. The adult client's survival story reflects unmet core emotional needs and the form of coping adaptation the child employed to deal with the childhood environment.

During this early phase of the counseling process, it is important to establish the nature of the broader core issue themes within the client's story. Counselor and client work together to develop an understanding of the core issue themes present in the client's survival story. Focusing on theses themes will aid the client's understanding of how the core issues specific to that client's life have been created and perpetuated over time. Core issue themes are rarely stated directly by the client. The counselor must listen for and reflect the salient components so the core need themes are made clear. White (1986) referred to this aspect of the counseling process as defining the specifications of personhood. He saw it as a crucial step because it frames the major limitations in how an individual adapts to new and different challenges.

So far the discussion has focused on the client and the childhood survival story. But it is important to recognize that the childhood survival story is created within the context of a large family story. Because the family is responsible for the child's initial culture influences, the family should never be underestimated when it comes to investigating the client's story. All family members hold a common understanding of the status quo and what must happen to maintain the homeostatic state. Family stories are often subtle and must be examined fully so the client can see how his or her own story has been influenced. This can also help the client to understand that the current story is just one part of an evolving process rather than being static and unchangeable. Counselor and client focus on the overall theme of the family story so that major characteristics of the family unit can be understood.

Task 2: Support the Client for Successfully Surviving the Powerlessness of Childhood

Although the ultimate goal is to help the client create a new and more productively adaptive story, personal truths are not given up easily. The counselor must provide support and praise for how well the client did in coping with the various situations that were part of the childhood environment. This approach avoids activating any form of protective resistance by the client to examining the elements of the story. Discussing the nature of the client's early life environment helps to reassure the client that he or she did the only thing that any child could do under the circumstances. This type of discussion can go a long way toward building rapport and sends a message that the counselor truly understands the difficulties the client endured.

Task 3: Connect the Common Elements of Core Issues Stories

As work with the client progresses, the counselor listens for the various elements of the core issue stories that emerge. This process starts with what the client reports as the current problem for which the client sought counseling services. As the client's history is gathered, a number of stories from the past will be told. Assessing the common elements of these stories (unmet core needs, coping style, trigger situations, and resulting thoughts, feelings, and behaviors) will help to clarify the assumptive truths the client has constructed about the self, others, and the nature of the world.

Task 4: Explore the Story From a Perspective External to the Self

If the client can observe his or her personal story much like one would view a film in a movie theater, the client can gain some objective perspective on the thoughts, feelings, and behaviors that have been problematic. A number of techniques can be employed to accomplish this part of the process. The counselor might ask the client to create a title for a recurring core issue story that has been identified. For example, a core issue story of abandonment might be titled "Alone and Unloved." The various roles the client plays at different times in the story can be labeled and referenced in the third person. This creates a frame of reference for these parts as characters in the client's story that the client takes on at various times. This conceptualization allows the client to more easily examine aspects of the self in process without mobilizing defenses that could truncate further exploration. The following dialogue with Bill, whose difficulty being at school and away from home was detailed earlier in the chapter, illustrates this technique.

> *Counselor:* So I am wondering, if this portion of your life were made into a movie, what might be a good title for the film?
> *Bill:* I don't know.
> *Counselor:* Right. I am sure you have never thought about this before. I am wondering, however, if we could just think about this some. So let me just tell you the story as I understand it and see if we can't come up with a short phrase that captures your story.
> *Bill:* Okay.
> *Counselor:* Here is the story as I understand it thus far. You were an excellent student in high school. You received admittance letters from every col-

lege to which you wished to go. You decided to come here, your first choice. You did very well academically your first semester despite the fact that you have been extremely depressed and anxious, have trouble sleeping, and feel really frightened. That is the story in a nutshell as I understand it. Would you agree?

Bill: Yeah.

Counselor: So if I were to tell you that story and ask to you come up with a title, what would it be?

Bill: I don't know. Maybe something like "The Life of a Loser!"

Counselor: Excellent. You have just given your story a title. We shall call it "The Life of a Loser."

Bill: What's so good about that?

Counselor: I was referring to the fact that you came up with a good title. Your question has me thinking that you either don't like that title or you don't like your story.

Bill: I hate that story. I don't want that story.

Counselor: Great. You have just established an important goal for yourself. You would like to change your story. That gives us a good starting place. To begin to change your story, however, we first need to get to know who the characters are in "The Life of a Loser."

Bill: That's the depressing part. There is just one character. That is me.

Counselor: Hmmm. I am sure it feels that way, but I am hearing something different. I am hearing about a number of roles that you play in your story.

Bill: What do you mean?

Counselor: Well, imagine that instead of just one Bill there are different parts that you play in your story. If you were watching a movie of this, they may all look like you, but each has a different role in bringing the story to life.

Bill: Yeah. There is me and messed up me.

Counselor: Right, only I am hearing more than just two of you. I think it might be useful if we can label each part of you in this story. So far I know about Good Student, Fearful Student, Stick It Out at School Student, and Feel Safe at Home Student. Would you disagree?

Bill: No. That sounds about right.

Counselor: So what we need to do is explore each of these roles and figure out what is going on with each of them. We have to figure out why it is that when you come to school, instead of feeling like Feel Safe at Home Student, Fearful Student comes to visit and takes over the whole show. If we can figure that out, we can then find ways to change those characters and ultimately change your story from "The Life of a Loser" to something more like "Having the Time of My Life at College."

This exchange shows how to work toward externalizing the story and objectifying the various roles that the client plays in the living story. This process can go a long way toward fostering an objective assessment of the self within the story. One of the major difficulties with living inside the core issue story is that it becomes a self-referenced way of being in, and relating to, the world. In other words, the client no longer makes a distinction between who he or she is as a person and the difficulties that are so much a part of the client's personal experience. The net effect is that the client's experience of self becomes fused with the history of problematic struggles the client has endured.

Unfortunately, the *DSM* system of diagnostic labeling used by much of the mental health industry reinforces negative "personal truth." For example, when a counselor says "You are an anorexic" or "He is a borderline," diagnosis is extended past labeling a psychiatric disorder to identifying the person as the disorder. Clients are not working in their own best interest when they think and label themselves as "being" depressed, anxious, bulimic, borderline, angry, violent, or any one of the many labels that may get attached to their struggle. One of the ways to counter this effect is to help the client reference the elements of the problem as individual entities that exist outside, and separate from, the self.

It is important to remember that prior to engaging the client in the process of externalizing, the client's problem story is not differentiated from the self. If the problem is fused with the self, the client often has a very difficult time perceiving the whole story and considering change. It is difficult to gain an objective view of that which surrounds you. If, however, the problem can be conceptualized as an entity in and of itself, the client can begin to think of it as possessing certain properties that can be differentiated from the self. The goal is to help the client consider the problem not as an aspect of the self but rather as this thing that causes problems for the self. If this can be done, counselor and client can join as a unified force with the goal of not letting the problem gain the upper hand. Given that the prime directive of all entities is to go on living, conceptualizing a problem as an entity suggests that it too will want to continue on in the client's life. The next logical question to be asked is, "How does this problem work to remain part of the client's life?" The goal here is to bring the client to consciously attend to the internal dynamics that keep the problem present. In most cases the client will not be able to provide direct answers to questions about how the problem maintains itself. This is a process of collaborative investigation in which counselor and client work together. This work often leads to new discoveries about the nature of problematic aspects of the client's life.

Task 5: Identify the Core Issue Trigger Points

The thoughts, feelings, and behaviors associated with a particular core issue are triggered as a result of specific situational conditions. By identifying the client's trigger points, the client can understand the elements that lead to personal vulnerability and develop the ability to manage core issue responses when they do occur. Having the client keep a core issues journal during the week will help identify situational conditions that make the client vulnerable. The journal entries should include the events leading up to the problematic episode, the thoughts, feelings, and behaviors that were triggered by the episode, the client's response to the triggered experience, and the consequences that followed. This and other similarly focused tasks help to increase the client's awareness of the core issue problem and enables the counselor to suggest specific short- and long-term counseling goals.

Task 6: Identify the Limitations of the Old Story

At this point counselor and client begin to look at how the elements of the client's survival story (the core issues and coping adaptation) no longer serve the client as well as they once did. When the client gets to this phase of the process, there is often quick recognition that the old ways of understanding self, others, or the nature of the world have resulted in some undesirable outcomes. Tying an overview of the client's history to the current reason for the client seeking counseling will help accomplish this task.

Task 7: Establish the Means to Stop Responding From the Old Story

This is the greatest challenge for the client in the overall change process. Recall that subjectively constructed truths serve as the basis upon which an individual establishes a known perspective for how life works. Giving up a personal truth is usually accomplished with some difficulty. The process is made easier when alternative truths can be experienced as in some way superior to the old truths.

From a narrative perspective, a number of intervention techniques can support the counselor and the client in this effort. Narrative theory suggests that one reason old stories remain strong is because the client is used to living within a set framework that focuses on the same supporting data and thus becomes more deeply embedded in the subjective "truth." One of the ways to intervene with stuck patterns is to compare and contrast the underlying elements upon which the client's truths have been established. The general goal of any intervention during this phase is to help make the thoughts and feelings that have been automatic responses to core issue triggers clearly conscious and open for revision. One effective intervention is to establish a new story based on personal preferences as opposed to the rigid beliefs that are no longer useful.

Engaging the client in a process in which new data are taken into account, alternative interpretations of that data are discussed, and different ways of understanding the whole story are developed helps loosen the client's hold on the status quo. Creating a level of cognitive dissonance around that which the client believes to be true can be very helpful in getting the client to tell different stories about a particular sequence of events. When the client is able to consider multiple ways of understanding a personal story, the counselor can assist the client in determining which of the stories feels most useful or best relates to how the client wishes to be. This process takes time, and the counselor should recognize that the client may demonstrate a propensity toward holding on to old truths, especially when exposed to stressful situations.

Task 8: Create a New Alternative Story

Over the course of this intervention process, the client will increasingly become aware of the various ways the old survival story, with its minefield of core issue problems, has been a major source for continued distress. The final task in the counseling process is to assist the client in creating a new story that provides a framework for more adaptive life responses. This portion of the process is aimed at tying the client's desired outcome goals to a new living story that is more adaptive.

Counselors are educated to focus on and discuss aspects of the client's life that are presented as problematic and to establish a diagnostic label for the symptoms presented. We might think of this process as telling the "abnormal," "pathological," or "problem" story. It is natural to focus on this dominant story because it usually carries with it intensity and pain. However, if the counselor does not actively engage in exploring exceptions to the dominant story, valuable data and opportunities to help the client's transition to a new story can be lost. It is important to remember that every story is created through a process of focusing on past experiences to the exclusion of other possible realities that could coexist with the dominant story. The goal is to help the client examine those other possibilities. This is not always an easy process. The client's early relational environment has set a schema in motion that filters out any information that is inconsistent with the client's relational view of the world. The counselor must constantly listen for situations in which the client is not living out the dominant story. These might be events wherein the client demonstrates signs of courage, strength, and compassion and an ability to adapt and change. Even if these times are brief and seemingly insignificant, it is important to examine each occurrence completely in the hope of building a framework for a new story. The ultimate goal in this phase of counseling is to help the client develop a new and more adaptive belief system that can be used to reassess the nature of self, others, and the world.

SUMMARY

This chapter provides a framework for the intervention phases that comprise the counseling process. This process begins with helping the client develop an understanding of the childhood survival story and how it is tied to the core problematic issues with which the client has struggled over time. Supporting the client's response to his or her childhood environment as a means of coping for survival enables counselor and client to build rapport and serves to help prevent the client from building an early defensive position. Connecting the common elements of the various core issue stories and clarifying the assumptive truths that have been constructed about the self, others, and the nature of the world allow the client's story to be expanded and understood as more than just an isolated problem. Examining the client's story as external to the self facilitates a greater degree of objective assessment of the problematic patterns that exist in the client's life. Identifying the core issue trigger points and understanding how those issues generate strong feelings, thoughts, and behaviors help the counselor create interventions that focus on the elements that fuel the problem. As the client identifies the limitations of this old, less adaptive story, the client can engage in an internal self-critique of the identified problems. Once the client has developed an appreciation for the types of specific elements that have been problematic, the counselor assists the client in establishing ways to stop responding from the core issue. At the same time, the client is encouraged to create new, more adaptive alternatives for understanding the nature of self, others, and the world.

CHAPTER 5

The Case of Sue

This chapter provides an example of both the assessment and treatment components of the core issues counseling model. Based on a 1-hour interview with a 38-year-old woman who initially presented with a martial problem, the interactions between counselor and client have been divided into segments. A brief core issues analysis of the case is presented between each segment as the interview progresses. The full treatment phase of the counseling process is not presented in this one interview, but the overview of a core issue assessment and some examples of intervention procedures consistent with the core issues counseling model will aid counselors in adapting this counseling approach to their own work.

BACKGROUND INFORMATION

Sue is a 38-year-old Caucasian female of German and Irish descent. She is a career woman of upper-middle socioeconomic status, and she has achieved that level of income herself through her own work. Currently, she works in a law practice and believes she is on a rapid career path that will lead to position advancement within her firm. Sue and her husband have been married for 8 years. They do not have children.

Sue had been working with another counselor, Martha, for the past 6 months to address problems in her marriage. During a supervision session, Martha stated that counseling sessions seem to have stalled with Sue and the limited progress that had been made has now stopped. The supervising counselor agreed to conduct a core issues assessment to see if additional insight could assist this client.

The client arrived for the interview on time and in casual clothing. She presents in a very formal manner that one could characterize as rigid or guarded. The interview begins with a standard intake format. Sue's counselor had already gathered some of the basic orienting information, so the consultant did not ask for this information again during the assessment.

SEGMENT 1:
INTAKE ORIENTING INFORMATION

Counselor: Hello Sue. What I'd like to do is have you tell me a little bit about what brought you in for counseling originally and essentially what you've been working on to this point.

Sue: Basically I first went to counseling because my husband and I were having a lot of marital difficulties. I mean, frankly, we were just not speaking to one another.

Counselor: Uh, hum.

Sue: There wasn't a lot of anger or upset. It was simply, you know, we didn't talk; we went our separate ways. And I really believed that this was something that he had to work at a little bit harder, but he would not seek counseling so I decided I would.

Counselor: Okay. So, if I understand you then, the relationship had kind of flatlined. There really wasn't a whole lot of excitement in the relationship or liveliness to it?

Sue: There wasn't a whole lot of conversation.

Counselor: Aha, aha. So the two of you weren't talking.

Sue: No.

Counselor: And just kind of leading separate lives in the same house.

Sue: Right.

Counselor: Had it always been that way, or was that different from before?

Sue: No. I mean we've been married 8 years, and in the beginning I think there was, you know, when you first get married and there's a lot of excitement and there's a lot of enthusiasm to sort of learn what one another is all about. And, I guess it just happened over time. We just sort of drifted apart.

Counselor: And what exactly have you been working on in counseling up to this point? When did you start, and what have you been focusing on?

Sue: I started about 6 months ago, and we've been talking primarily about why I am where I am today and what has brought me to this point.

Counselor: Over that time, what have you focused on in counseling.

Sue: A lot about my childhood and my parents and stuff like that.

Counselor: All right, good. What I'd like to do is find out a little bit more about you, sort of get the big picture of what you do for work, what your social life is like, and those types of things. Would that be all right?

Sue: Uh-huh.

Counselor: Okay. Let's start with your education. Can you tell me a little bit about your educational background?

Sue: Uh-huh. I have my law degree and an undergraduate degree in finance.

Counselor: And did you go right on to law school or work for a time?

Sue: No. I went to law school immediately upon graduation.

Counselor: And you're practicing now?

Sue: Yes I am.

Counselor: What type of law?

Sue: Corporate law.

Counselor: And where are you on the career ladder?

Sue: Well, I hope to make Vice President within the next few years. And I would be one of the youngest and the only female to make Vice President in this particular firm.

Counselor: Okay. And as you went through school, did you achieve pretty good grades?

Sue: Very, very good grades.

Counselor: And what other types of achievements have you accomplished over your time either in school or outside of school, other areas?

Sue: Oh, I don't know, I put a lot of time and effort into my studies. I'm not sure there was much else besides that. I danced for years and did horseback riding and competed a little bit.

Counselor: But your studies were primary?

Sue: They were. Uh-huh.

Counselor: And what about other social relationships? Can you tell me a little bit about those?

Sue: Like friends? [*hint of sarcasm in her manner when posing this question*]

Counselor: Yeah.

Sue: Friends. My friends are mostly my colleagues. I don't have a lot of friends for socializing outside of the office. So the friends I have are those people that I come into contact with every day. We eat lunch together, we work out in the gym together.

Counselor: Uh-huh.

Sue: We run in the morning together, but aside from that I can't say. [*pause*] I have acquaintances, but I don't have many close friends.

Counselor: Okay. And your family? Are your parents still living?

Sue: Yes.

Counselor: Do you see them frequently or . . . ?

Sue: Infrequently.

Counselor: Is that a geographic situation or due to some other reason?

Sue: They live about 2 hours from here, but basically they're very involved in their own lives still, and you know, we try to work weekends out occasionally but it's very stilted and uncomfortable, and I don't think they particularly want to be around me. So, you know . . .

Counselor: Has that always kind of been the situation in your family, or is that a more recent development?

Sue: No, my parents and I have never been particularly close.

Counselor: Can you tell me a little bit about them? How long they've been married, and do you have brothers and sisters?

Sue: They've been married a long time, I don't know, 40 years I guess. I don't really keep track. My mom's a biochemist, and my dad is a physician, a pediatrician. They are both very bright, very motivated, and very involved in their careers.

Counselor: Uh, hum.

Sue: And I have a sister 19 months younger than me.

Counselor: And where is she right now?

Sue: She lives in the same town my parents live in.

Counselor: And is she working in a profession as well?

Sue: Yeah, she is, she's an elementary school teacher.

Counselor: Do you have a lot of contact with her?

Sue: No.

Analysis of Segment 1

The first segment begins as a standard intake interview that follows a psychosocial format. In addition to being sure that each area of intake information is gathered, focusing on a broad-based psychosocial format tends to prompt details of the client's story. This client has provided some interesting initial information. Sue reports that she sought counseling services to address problems in her marriage, which, after 8 years, seems to be slowly failing to keep the couple engaged with each other. Further, when questioned about social friendships, Sue reports having few, if any, friends. The focus on interpersonal relationships with her work associates and a lack of involvement with her family of origin bring up some material that suggests a distance from parents and family. The picture that leaps out, in just the first few minutes of the interview, is that this woman seems to be socially isolated in some significant areas of her life. From a core issues perspective, the key question the counselor needs to keep in mind early in the interview process is, "What would account for this client's lack of relational connection?" Listening for material around which the counselor can glean the broader core issue domains always helps to answer that question. Although information was not gathered to construct a multigenerational genogram for this client, doing so may aid the counselor in assessing the nature of relational patterns within the family of origin (A. Berg, 1991; McGoldrick, Gerson, & Shellenberger, 1999).

SEGMENT 2:
RELATIONSHIP HISTORY WITH SPOUSE

Counselor: So, what about your husband? What does he do?

Sue: He's also an attorney. He works for a nonprofit corporation and spends a lot of hours at work as well.

Counselor: Uh, hum. And you said you met 8 years ago. Where? Did you meet in law school or college?

Sue: We met in law school.

Counselor: You met in law school.

Sue: We were always on the same kind of track.

Counselor: Uh, hum. So at an earlier point there was a time perhaps when the two of you were talking a lot about your work and you were kind of on the same track and supporting each other that way?

Sue: Right.

Counselor: Do you remember the types of things that first attracted you to your husband?

Sue: Well, I loved his ambition. I loved the fact that he really wanted to do something that made a difference, and he was always very kind to me. He brought me flowers, did little things that were really special, and made me feel really special. I think that's what it was.

Counselor: As you were saying that, you were smiling. What kind of feelings did thinking about those times bring up for you?

Sue: It made me feel like I was worth something [*strong emphasis in her voice*]. If he could care about me and love me enough to do just really nice little things for me, it meant I was worth something. Like take me away for a weekend unexpectedly. I didn't have to make any of the reservations. I didn't have to do any of the planning. Or he'd bake a cake for my birthday, which was just really special. So that made me feel like maybe I was a worthwhile individual. I would call that an achievement.

Counselor: Call what an achievement?

Sue: That someone like that could love me.

Counselor: So you saw this man was very special who gave you a lot of attention and really filled a need that you had.

Sue: Yeah, I would say so.

Counselor: Okay. And if you could put a label on that need, what would you call it?

Sue: Love.

Counselor: Love?

Sue: Yeah, I think I needed to be loved. And he was the first person I ever felt really did that.

Analysis of Segment 2

In this segment of the interview, information about the client's relationship history with her husband unfolds. Both the content of the client's report and the manner in which she reported the information suggest that she responded very positively when someone showed he cared about her. From a core issues perspective, the counselor would focus attention on statements such as "He was really kind to me." "He made me feel really special—like I was worth something—like I was a worthwhile individual," and "I needed to be loved, and he was the first person I ever felt really did that."

Given the relational isolation the client had reported in other areas of her life and the emphasis on needing to be loved, the counselor begins to consider core issue domains that might fit these data. If emotional connection and love was an unmet core emotion, then a reasonable hypothesis could be formed around the existence of problems within the core issue domain of Disconnection and Rejection.

SEGMENT 3:
THE CLIENT'S EARLY LIFE

Counselor: Let's talk a little bit more about some of the things that happened within your family and trace your earlier years up through college.

Sue: Yeah, we were what I would call, and I'm learning this, you know, from being in therapy, a pretty dysfunctional family.

Counselor: Dysfunctional. What does that mean to you?

[*It is always important to have a client define "catch" terms and phrases and not make assumptions about what those terms mean to a client.*]

Sue: Well, that my parents were around rarely. We had a series of nannies and au pairs and live-in housekeepers that took care of my sister and me. You know, we never sat down for dinner together. That's not true. Sometimes my parents would have friends over and then, you know, somehow we had this family dinner, but it was always with other people there.

Counselor: Uh, hum.

Sue: I was very much alone. I spent a lot of time in my room. I read voraciously. We weren't really allowed to have other friends over because it was very disruptive to the household, and growing up with a series of caretakers, most of whom I knew for only, I don't know, you know, 6 months to a year. The rules were never the same. There was never any consistency.

Analysis of Segment 3

In this segment more information about the client's early life emerges. At this point in the interview, the information provides an initial confirmation of a possible core issue in the Disconnection and Rejection domain. The client states that her parents were for the most part unavailable and that she felt alone. The children in the family had multiple caretakers, and there was some suggestion that there was a lack of consistency as these caretakers rotated in and out of the home. From a core issues perspective, the counselor would now look toward developing hypotheses regarding specific core issues that might be in play. The information presented thus far suggests a core issue of emotional deprivation may be present. Recall that a core issue of emotional deprivation can arise if the client has expectations that her emotional needs will not be adequately met by others. Young (1999) offered specific aspects of emotional support that may have been deprived. These include nurturance, protection, and empathy. It is important to remember that the counselor has only constructed hypotheses about the client's core issue. The next step is to determine how much or how little support there is for the initial core issue hypothesis that has been made.

SEGMENT 4:
CLIENT'S SURVIVAL STORY

Counselor: It's interesting to me that some people might look at your life, your success in the law profession, being an up and coming Vice President at your firm, as being a lot of success, and yet I don't get the sense that you see it the same way. Is that accurate?

Sue: It's because I don't feel like what I have done is a success. I mean, I did what I had to do. You know? I concentrated on doing my studies and being academically excellent. I had nothing else. So I never feel it was anything that I did. It's almost like I didn't have choices. So I was sort of pushed in this direction out of what I really believe was a protective kind of thing for myself. So I still don't believe it's anything I accomplished. Or the accomplishment isn't mine.

Analysis of Segment 4

In this segment the client's survival story narrative emerges from the content of the session. As presented earlier, the survival story reflects the need for safety as perceived by the child and with conditions within the environment that determine what must be done in order to ensure that level of safety (Parry & Doan, 1994). The survival story is usually expressed as an "if-then" statement: If I do _____, then I will survive.

Sue describes her situation with statements such as "I did what I had to do," "It is as if I didn't have any choices." and "A protective kind of thing for myself so the accomplishment isn't mine." The assessment process is aided if the counselor can help the client articulate the survival story in greater detail so that the various elements of that story can be examined during later stages of the counseling process.

SEGMENT 5:
DETAILS OF THE CLIENT'S SURVIVAL STORY

Counselor: You said you did the things that you had to do. Can you tell me more about that, and give me a list of those things that you had to do?

Sue: Yeah. I mean if I didn't bring home As on my report card, it was probably the only time, the only interest my parents took in me. If I didn't bring home As, then they were terribly disappointed and often just wouldn't speak to me for weeks at a time. I was very isolated anyway, and the other kids at school, I never seemed to be able to relate to them. As I said, I couldn't, you know, my parents really didn't allow me to form close relationships with other students. I couldn't have them over for sleepovers and all this stuff kids normally do, so I just set my agenda and that was it. I used to say, for example, I used to say, I can read two fiction books in a week if I read three nonfiction books. And I would do this. That was my discipline. That was my way of coping.

Counselor: So you really set criteria for yourself.

Sue: Oh, yeah. Oh, yeah.

Counselor: And then tried to measure up to the criteria that you set.

Sue: Absolutely! And if I fell short, I would punish myself. I would starve myself for 2 days, or I would make myself eat things I didn't like. Or, you know, I would not take a bath for 2 days. So I set my own standards there too. My parents really did not have to tell me or punish me because I did it to myself.

Counselor: One of the things you said was that you couldn't have other children over as friends because they would make too much noise.

Sue: Right.

Counselor: Were there rigid standards that were set around quietness in the house and a lot of rules about what you do and you don't do?

Sue: Yeah. Because if my parents were home, they were working. And they each had their own study, and they wanted to be by themselves. They couldn't even stand the sound of the television. Yeah, we just had to adhere to the rules.

Counselor: I get the sense that that was very lonely for you? Would that be correct?

Sue: Yeah, it was lonely.

Counselor: Lonely, okay.

Analysis of Segment 5

In this segment the survival story is filled out in more detail. The client states, "If I didn't bring home As . . . they wouldn't speak to me." From this statement is seems clear the client understood that approval and connection with her parents, at least in part, was contingent upon her academic achievement. There is also some further confirmation of the client's experience of emotional deprivation in her statements about feeling isolated as a child.

If, at this point in the interview, the counselor were to tentatively accept that at least one of the client's core issues is emotional deprivation, the counselor needs to attend to how that core issue is expressed. The three broad coping strategies that a client may employ in the face of a core issue once it has been triggered are compensation adaptation, avoidance adaptation, and surrender adaptation. Each of these forms of coping adaptation is expressed in one or more of three relational dimensions: relationship with self, relationship with others, or relationship with the nature of the world.

In segment 5 the client provides some initial indication that she uses a compensation adaptation coping strategy in the face of emotional deprivation. She stated, "I just set my agenda and that was it." It will be important from this point forward to listen for evidence that supports or refutes the contention that the client applies this strategy consistently in her life.

Finally, there was some preliminary probing regarding a secondary core issue around the rigid nature of the home environment and the rules with which the client grew up. This probing centered on the hypothesis that the client may also struggle with the core issue of unrelenting standards. Recall that the core issue of unrelenting standards exists in the domain of Overvigilance and Inhibition. A client who struggles with the core issue of unrelenting standards tends to operate out of the sense that there is a right way to do everything. There is also rigidity about rules, and these clients strive to meet internalized standards at the expense of their own gratification, often with an emphasis placed on one or more areas of success. The counselor will want to remain attentive to any further information that supports or refutes the existence of this second core issue.

SEGMENT 6:
FAILURE TO MEET CORE NEEDS

Sue: And I never had to work outside the home. I never had to have a job. So, you know, I just pretty much would come home from school every afternoon and go to my room and start studying.

Counselor: And start studying.

Sue: Yeah.

Counselor: Were your parents pleased with your academic performance? Did they ever show you any indication that they were pleased?

Sue: Maybe. I suppose, you know. I mean, that's what they expected, so if that equates to pleasure, I guess they were pleased.

Counselor: So you tried to at least meet the expectations that they had if not exceed them.

Sue: Oh yeah. But I'm not sure I ever did. Because they never really let me know.

Counselor: Was there ever a time that you didn't meet achievement expectations and your parents let you know they were not pleased?

Sue: Yeah, there were those few times when I would get Bs in English class, I remember, and once in a Social Studies class, and you would have thought, you know, I had committed a serious crime. I remember I was so humiliated because my mother, who had never ever set foot in my school ever, I mean she never came to any of the functions, set up a meeting with both of these teachers to find out what had happened, and, you know, basically it was just humiliating. She told them that, you know, it was probably something they had done. That they were probably very bad teachers and would they consider tendering their resignations. I mean, it was just so outrageous, and I didn't even know how I was going to be able to face them after that. So those two things I remember really clearly.

Counselor: So your mother not only had expectations for you but also expectations for others who you came in contact with or others around her?

Sue: Oh yes.

Analysis of Segment 6

In this segment the client shares that despite her efforts to do what she believed might help to satisfy her need for love and affection, it did not work. Speaking of her parents' expectations, she stated, "I am not sure I ever met them because they never let me know." Sue's mother's reaction to less than acceptable grades in high school lends support to the idea of unrelenting standards as an additional core issue with which this client struggles.

SEGMENT 7:
CLIENT'S RELATIONSHIP HISTORY

Counselor: What I'd like to do is ask you now a little bit about dating relationships in high school and on through college. Did you date in high school?

Sue: No, not really. A friend of mine and I went to our senior prom together, just because we thought we should go to the senior prom. But no, it was not, not really a date. In college it was much the same. I had some friendships that, you know, sort of might have started out to be romantically inclined, but it didn't go anywhere.

Counselor: Uh, hum. Was that because you weren't interested? Or did they lose interest?

Sue: Yeah. Well, I don't know. I think both ways.

Counselor: Both ways.

Sue: Yeah.

Counselor: And what about law school then?

Sue: Well, that's where I met my husband. And we were in the same year and some classes together, but I never really noticed him. But one day I was in the law library studying and all of a sudden someone, who happened to be him, put a flower on top of the book I was reading, and I looked up and he said, "I was just wondering if you'd like to go for coffee with me?" And that's how we met.

Counselor: Uh, hum. Can you think back to that time, what the feeling was that you had?

Sue: I was amazed. I was, and I didn't really know how to respond. My first inclination was to push him away and say, you know, "I don't have time," "I don't know you," but for some reason I was just really touched by that gesture. I just felt like, you know, it was okay to say yes. So I did.

Counselor: How did the relationship progress from there?

Sue: Well, I've got to tell you that I still fought it. I mean, he was wooing me from the start I think. Although we didn't have much money at that time, he would save money to take me out to a nice restaurant. He would just show up at my door with flowers, wildflowers, or whatever. Or he'd come early in the morning and say, "Come on, let's take a hike together." And so I just kind of, I guess, I just kind of let it happen. Although I remember a time, early on, that for weeks he would call and I would let the answering machine pick up. I wouldn't take his phone call because I was scared.

Counselor: What were you scared of at that time? Do you have a sense about that?

Sue: Well, for one thing I think I was really falling in love with him, and I was petrified of disappointing him. I thought, you know, if he really gets to know the real me, he's not going to like me very much. I remember thinking that it was better to have him leave now thinking that I was this great person than pursue a relationship and have him be disappointed in me.

Counselor: So that was a major fear, the fear that you might not measure up to his standards. Is that right?

Sue: Yeah.

Counselor: All right. And you got married, so I'm assuming you were able to kind of push through that fear enough to act on your love for him.

Sue: Yeah.

Counselor: How did that happen?

Sue: I don't even know.

Counselor: Not sure.

Sue: Yeah. I mean, I think that I finally said, as I said he was so kind and so wonderful and so gentle that I just kept saying, you know, I believe that I can do this. I believe that I'm good enough. I believe that, you know, I believe that I'm worthy of being loved.

Counselor: Uh, hum.

Sue: And I did love him. So yeah. We went for it.

Analysis of Segment 7

In this segment the focus is shifted from the client's family of origin to the client's relationship history. Specific emphasis was placed on an initial investigation of the client's history with her husband. As this segment unfolds, a new and interesting element comes to light. The client has truly been warmed by interactions with her husband, especially at times when he was attentive. When he placed the flower on the book she was reading, she remembers, "For some reason I was really touched by that gesture." This could speak to the experience of having another individual show caring and affection that she was deprived of in childhood. Rather than expressing the core issue with an approach like compensation adaptation, however, the client employs an avoidance adaptation. She states, "I fought it, and I was scared." Also emerging further in this segment is the second core issue of unrelenting standards. "I was falling in love with him, and I was petrified of disappointing him. If he really gets to know the real me, he is not going to like me very much." This is similar to some content that emerged in segment 5. In situations that trigger core issues relating to deprivation of nurturance, Sue employs an avoidance adaptation coping response. These are the kinds of thematic patterns that the counselor must look for and come to understand. This understanding of the client's relational world will allow the counselor to successful join the client in her relational struggle (Chu, 1992).

SEGMENT 8:
CORE ISSUE EXPRESSED AS THE ADULT LIVING STORY

Counselor: Can you trace through the different periods of your marriage that have led up to this point in you life?

Sue: Yeah. As I said, in the beginning it was much the same as the courting stage, everything was champagne at night occasionally and long walks.

He'd read to me wonderful poems that he wrote. Sometimes he would leave little cards in my briefcase that said "I love you." I don't know. It's so hard for me to pin down. I keep going back, and initially I thought this is me, this must have been something I did. This must have been something I created, because all of a sudden I was working really long hours and he was working really long hours and we were both exhausted. And then I just kind of began to feel again this apprehension that maybe, you know, what made me think this could ever work to begin with? What made me think that I could have this kind of relationship with someone? So I moved into the other bedroom, and he'd ask me why, and I'd say, "Because, you know, I just need some space right now." And he'd ask and he'd ask, and then finally he stopped asking. It's so strange because we do live in the same house, and we drink coffee together in the morning. We have a dog that we share responsibilities for. We still have acquaintances over sometimes for dinner, and we're a couple. I don't know if he's talking to anyone, but, you know, the first person I ever talked to about it was when I went to counseling.

Counselor: So, it sounds as though there is not only the fear that you had to push through to make the relationship happen, but later on it sounds like that fear came in once again and has served to essentially seal you off from him to some degree. Would that be accurate?

Sue: Yes.

Counselor: Your husband asked you what was happening, and your response was that you weren't sure, you just needed to have some space. Was that the most definite answer you could come up with at the time, or was there something behind that that you didn't feel comfortable sharing?

Sue: I guess I was really afraid for him to see my weaknesses, and I think one of my big weaknesses is the fact that I can't maintain relationships. I don't know how to do it.

Counselor: Uh, hum.

Sue: I was really afraid that if I said to him, "I need some help with this. I know I'm screwing this up, but I don't know how to do it," then again he would say, "Oh, you know, this is a person I didn't know, you know, this person has a lot of weaknesses and needs, and I certainly don't need anybody dependent." I mean, I think that one of the reasons he loved me is because of my independence, and so I was so fearful of showing him a weaker side. So it was easier to just back off and close myself away from him than to admit that I was feeling something that was pretty scary to me.

Counselor: If I understand it correctly, there is this strength that is of value and that is what you put out to the world. There is that strong competent woman who gets out there and makes it all happen. She really has been your major ally and has allowed you to achieve all the things that you've achieved. That strength actually helped you survive your childhood to some degree. That strength says to be strong, to be independent, not to need people, to get along on your own. Is that right?

Sue: Yes.

Counselor: Yet underneath, or on the inside of this strong exterior, there are weaknesses as well, and those are things that need to be covered up, to be hidden, and not allow other people to see from the outside.

Sue: [*nods affirmatively, eyes begin to fill with tears*]

Counselor: It also sounds like, at this point, the part of you that is the stronger is actually pushing your husband away in order to hide the weak part, is that right?

Sue: [*nods again affirmatively and begins to weep*]

Counselor: It looks like getting in touch with this is upsetting for you.

Sue: [*sobbing*] You know, the thing that's really upsetting is that I really love him, and I really believe that he loves me. He's the one person in my life that I really feel like I've been able to trust, and I'm screwing it up. Then I think, you know, and I wouldn't blame him. What if he's seeing someone else? What if, and for all I want to tell him all these things, I can't. That's the part that's really hard [*continues to cry*].

Counselor: Uh, hum. It looks like it is very hard for you right now.

Analysis of Segment 8

This is a particularly interesting portion of the interview in that the client's core issue is expressed within the context of the client's adult living story. At long last the client has established a meaningful relationship with an individual who can show her love and affection. This could go a long way toward helping the client heal the hurtful relational wounds that resulted from the emotional deprivation she suffered at an earlier time in her life. Yet this path of love and caring is not one that is especially comfortable for her. She states, "I began to feel this apprehension. What made me think this could ever work? I was really afraid for him to see my weaknesses."

Once the client identifies her feelings of discomfort as weaknesses, the core issue of unrelenting standards is triggered, and she begins to project onto her husband the response of a disapproving other. "If I say to him I need some help with this, he would say this person has weaknesses, and I certainly don't need anybody dependent." Sue has identified this set of feelings as weaknesses and fears that she will, at long last, be found out. An avoidance adaptation coping style is then employed as a means of keeping her from experiencing the feelings associated with the emotional deprivation core issue. The avoidance adaptation allows Sue to stay away from her emotional discomfort.

At this point in the interview, Sue begins to experience her sadness. This sadness is expressed in tears when her survival story is reflected back to her. This segment of the interview captures the process of the client's coping styles in the face of the two core issues that have been hypothesized so far. Sue's strong exterior pushes her husband away in order to hide parts of herself that she has identified as weak and not up to acceptable standards for herself or others. In doing so, Sue provides an example of avoidance adaptation in response to both core issues—emotional deprivation and unrelenting standards. Upon hearing this reflection, the client becomes tearful. This tearful response can be understood as the painful emotions attached to her emotional deprivation that are being triggered at this point in the interview. This is a very interesting development in that Sue is expressing feelings and is now showing that unacceptable side of herself that she does not want others to see. The immediate in-session goal is to stay with the affective content and explore her feeling state in an attempt to form a better understanding of her emotional experience.

SEGMENT 9:
CLIENT REVEALS THINKING PROCESS
ABOUT PARTS OF SELF

Counselor: Can you tell me what you're feeling right now?

Sue: Yeah. I'm feeling really sad and really alone. And I'm feeling really scared.

Counselor: Are those the things that are attached to the weak side?

Sue: Yeah.

Counselor: Can you tell me a little bit more about the weak part?

Sue: Yeah, I mean, most of the people that I work with I'm sure call me names behind my back that aren't very nice. You know, the iron maiden, the ice queen, always in control, you know, never let my emotions come through. But underneath there are so many times when even though I'm portraying this really tough image, that I want to just say, you know, I'm not feeling this. I'm scared. I'm going to trial, and I'm petrified. My knees are shaking. Or I've somehow gotten emotionally involved, and I want to be able to talk about that.

Counselor: Uh, hum.

Sue: But you know there's something that says "no you can't, you have to be above all that; you have to be above emotions; you have to get rid of all those insignificant thoughts and feelings that just get in the way of doing your job." [*With this one statement the client stops crying immediately.*]

Counselor: Uh, hum. So there's kind of a discounting of the emotional side.

Sue: Right.

Counselor: The softer side.

Sue: Yeah, right. That's right.

Counselor: So there's an aspect of you that discounts and devalues that feeling, and there is another part of you that sees the importance of having these feelings. Both of these parts are present within you and make you who you are.

Analysis of Segment 9

In this segment Sue reveals how the parts of herself that have been identified operate. The segment starts out with an inquiry into her feeling state, which she is able to readily identify. Sue states, "I'm feeling really sad, really alone, and really scared." These are the feelings attached to what Sue labels the "weak" part, which provides further validation for emotional deprivation being at least one of the client's core issues. The next instant, however, Sue seals up all of her emotional expression as she begins to talk about a part of her that says, "You have to be above emotions, get rid of insignificant thoughts and feelings that get in the way." One might conclude that this message is coming from the core issue of unrelenting standards. This is the part that the client has identified as the "strong" part, which literally pushes the emotional or "weak" part away in an effort to live up to an idealized standard.

SEGMENT 10:
VERIFICATION OF CORE ISSUE
AND BEGINNING TO RE-AUTHOR LIFE STORY

Sue: I mean, I still think that I would love to go home and have my mother hold me.

Counselor: Uh, hum.

Sue: And tell me that I'm okay and that she loves me because of who I am, not because of what I do.

Counselor: Uh, hum.

Sue: I know that won't happen so . . .

Counselor: Uh, hum. And if that could happen? Let's say you woke up tomorrow, and overnight a miracle happened . . .

Sue: It would take a miracle [*laughs*].

Counselor: Okay, well, let's say that that did happen. Only you didn't know that a miracle had happened. In what ways would your life be different? What would be some of the indications that something had happened?

Sue: I would be able to believe that I am a worthwhile person, that who I am inside is greater than the sum of my behaviors and my actions.

Counselor: Uh, hum.

Sue: That I would be able to love without being fearful of not getting that love in return.

Counselor: Uh, hum.

Sue: That I would get pregnant, that I would want a baby of my own, that I would just be happy and content with me.

Counselor: Uh, hum. So I get the sense that your life would fill out; it wouldn't be resting primarily on your career success. It would be a much fuller encompassing of all the experiences that are available?

Sue: Right.

Counselor: Okay. Uh, hum.

Analysis of Segment 10

Segment 10 provides final verification that the core issue of emotional deprivation is an area with which this client struggles. The client's deprivation of nurturance is clearly captured when she states, "What I would love to do is go home and have my mother hold me and have her tell me that she loves me because of what I am and not because of what I do."

This segment also shows the beginning of the process to assist the client in re-authoring the story. Here the counselor asks what is known as the "miracle question" (I. Berg & Miller, 1992; de Shazer, 1988; White & Espton, 1990). The miracle question asks the client to look into a future frame and view the client's life condition. It provides a basis for helping to co-construct goals with the client and orient the focus of counseling sessions. According to I. Berg and Miller (1992), the miracle question is asked as follows:

> Suppose that one night, while you were asleep, there is a miracle and the problem that brought you into therapy is solved. However, because you are asleep you don't know the miracle has happened. When you wake up in the morning, what will be different that will tell you that this miracle has taken place? (p. 13)

Sue's response to this question addresses three major areas where her life would be different: (1) she would be able to believe that who she is inside is a worthwhile person, (2) she would be able to love without being fearful of not getting that love in return, and (3) she would take the major step of getting pregnant and wanting a baby. Sue believes that taking these three steps would result in a greater degree of happiness and contentment in her life. Each of these changes could be marked out as longer term goals that the client has advanced. The move now is to help the client understand the nature of the work that must be accomplished to create and begin living out a new story that is adaptive to her core issues story in a different way. The goal here is to help the client construct a framework that will allow her to respond in different ways when her core issues are triggered. An important step early in the counseling process is externalizing the old story, which is done by labeling different parts of the client that are played out in her story. Helping the client provide information regarding the detailed nature of each part as the story unfolds assists greatly in helping the client understand the process of her story.

SEGMENT 11:
LABELING THE VARIOUS ROLES
IN THE CLIENT'S STORY

Counselor: Well, I'm curious about these parts of you, the very competent achieving part and then this softer side. If you were to label these parts of yourself, what would be accurate labels that you might be able to come up with to name them?

Sue: Well it's my external.

Counselor: Your external.

Sue: Right, and my internal.

Counselor: Okay.

Sue: It's the external part that I share with everyone . . .

Counselor: Uh, hum.

Sue: . . . and the internal is the part I don't share with anyone.

Counselor: Uh, hum. And there's also kind of some judging that goes along with, or judgments that are made about, those different parts.

Sue: Yup.

Counselor: What would you say the judgments are about each one, the external Sue, the internal Sue?

Sue: That the external is acceptable and expected and right.

Counselor: Uh, hum.

Sue: And the internal is weak and pathetic and needy.

Counselor: Uh, hum. Okay. It just strikes me that the external has all positives and the internal has all negatives. That comes across pretty clearly.

Sue: Yeah.

Counselor: Are there also some negatives that you see relative to the external Sue, and are there any positive aspects to the internal Sue?

Sue: Six months ago I would have said no. But, yeah, the external side is a facade, is phony, I mean not totally, but who I think I should be.

Counselor: Okay.

Sue: And the internal side is maybe who I am and has the capacity to love.

Counselor: Uh, hum.

Sue: And to reach out to others.

Counselor: Okay. This side has the capacity to do that but not the tools, perhaps, to do that? I mean, the capacity is one thing, but actually being able to do that is another.

Sue: That's right. I mean, not only am I afraid of doing it, I don't know how to do it.

Counselor: Okay. All right.

Sue: Yeah.

Counselor: Uh, hum. And I'm wondering about the process of this also. I am wondering if we could go through a scenario of a time that the internal Sue kind of comes to visit a situation, what the external Sue does to her when that happens. Can you pick a time that has happened recently and help me understand what the process is when these two people come to meet one another around a situation?

Sue: Yup. I can think of one that happened not too long ago. One of my colleagues was pregnant. We were going to court together, and she had a miscarriage in her ninth week. And the trial was scheduled for the next day, and the internal Sue wanted to go to her house, take her chicken soup, and say, you know, "Kathy, don't worry about it. You know this is obviously so traumatic and so awful for you, and you come back when you feel like coming back."

Counselor: Uh, hum.

Sue: And the external Sue said, "No, you know you have a job to do, and I certainly, if I were going through this, I would be at that trial the next day, and so Kathy I expect that of you too."

Counselor: Uh, hum.

Sue: So yeah.

Counselor: Okay. So this is the external Sue and the internal Sue in their reference to Kathy.

Sue: Right.

Counselor: What about the external Sue and the internal Sue in reference to each other? Is there a dialogue between these two?

Sue: Yeah, like when I'm walking into a meeting and my knees are shaking and I'm feeling really not very sure of myself.

Counselor: Uh, hum.

Sue: And so the internal me will be saying, "I'm really scared, you know this is really pretty overwhelming. What if I screw up?" And the external Sue is saying, "Don't be silly, don't be such an ass, go in there, you know you know your stuff, just do it and don't feel insecure about it."

Counselor: Uh, hum.

Sue: And, oh, they talk to each other all the time. Yeah.

Counselor: Uh, hum. Okay. And how would the internal Sue respond to that?

Sue: She would back down.

Counselor: She would back down. Uh, hum.

Sue: She'd say, "You're right."

Counselor: Uh, hum.

Analysis of Segment 11

As the counselor helps Sue explore aspects of herself by labeling different parts that get played out in her life, it is interesting to see how Sue identifies these parts as existing as dualistic in nature. Getting a client to label different parts or roles that are being played out assists the process of helping the client to externalize the living story. In this case the client labels these parts internal Sue and external Sue. It will be important to use these labels and reference them using third-person language. Doing so serves to frame aspects of the self as independent role entities and thereby externalize them. The externalization of her story's characters can assist Sue in developing effective strategies for making changes in the future.

At this point in the interview Sue is making an assessment of these two parts from "external" Sue's point of view. She comes out with absolute positives for the external standards-oriented part of herself and absolute negatives for the internal feeling-oriented part of herself. There is, of course, a high probability that she actually does experience these parts of herself as being as extreme as she has characterized them. In fact, the lack of a middle ground is a major part of this client's problem. Therefore, the counselor must confront Sue's characterization of these parts as extreme and polarized. Very often clients will need help in doing this, but Sue was able to articulate a more balanced position quite easily. The main point here is that helping the client to explore the parts being played out in the story is important in that it is unlikely that such exploration will take place without the counselor's assistance. Effectively assisting the client in this process is a first step toward getting her to consider more than one perspective for her story. Helping the client consider additional perspectives of her story is what will ultimately allow for the construction of a new living story.

The next step is to help the client understand the connection between how she responds in these differing relational situations and the core issues with which she struggles. This is accomplished by tracing the process of her story and making finer and finer distinctions in the roles that are played out during her interactions with others.

SEGMENT 12:
HELPING THE CLIENT EXPAND HER LIVING STORY

Counselor: There's something that strikes me about your description of internal Sue that I'm wondering about. That is, when you talk about the positive parts of internal Sue, the capacities she has to care and nurture, that didn't sound the same as when you talk about going into a meeting. It doesn't sound like those are the qualities that are present at the time. I'm wondering if there might not be another part that's happening or another part of the internal Sue that you haven't shared yet. There is a worried, threatened, and scared part that I hear. Is that part of the internal Sue as well?

Sue: Yup.

Counselor: Okay. And can you tell me a little bit more about that?

Sue: I mean, it's just that I'm so afraid of screwing up. And so afraid of failure.

Counselor: Uh, hum.

Sue: I've taken risks in my life, I really have.

Counselor: Uh, hum.

Sue: Not with relationships really, but certainly in my professional career. So I've taken risks. It's not that I'm so afraid that I don't take the risks, but I live my life in fear that I'm going to fail.

Counselor: Uh, hum.

Sue: That I'm not going to live up to the expectations that are there.

Counselor: Uh, hum.

Sue: And, yeah, that's really scary.

Counselor: Okay. And that also sounds a little bit like the time that you wanted to reach out to your husband and you pulled back. That somehow there were inadequacies or that a fear of failing to live up to expectations kept you from doing it.

Sue: That's exactly right. That's exactly right.

Counselor: Uh, huh.

Sue: If he finds out who I really am, he won't love me because I won't meet his expectations.

Counselor: Okay. So it really sounds like there's kind of three different parts to this story. There's the external Sue, the loving Sue, and the fearful Sue. And I guess I wonder about the external–internal piece because one sounds like it's on the outside of you and the other sounds like it's on the inside of you.

Sue: Uh, hum.

Counselor: And I'm wondering if there are three aspects, all of which are on the inside but essentially take turns, or kind of, don't exist all at once at the same time.

Sue: Uh, hum.

Counselor: Is that an inaccurate description?

Sue: No, I think that, I actually think that makes sense.

Counselor: Okay.

Sue: Yeah.

Counselor: All right.

Analysis of Segment 12

Listening to the process of the story will often reveal greater complexity than the client is initially aware of and able to articulate. The counselor must help the client expand on the story and go into greater detail about every significant role encompassed by the story. Carefully exploring and labeling each role of the client's story as well as the process of how that story unfolds is the key to helping the client achieve change-related goals. Conceptually, from a narrative perspective, the ultimate goal is to enable the client to reconstruct the nature and meaning of her own living story (Catford & Ray, 1991; Hardy, 1977; Howard, 1989; Nussbaum, 1988; Parry & Doan, 1994; Polkinghorne, 1988; Wanner, 1994).

The difficult challenge is that the client is embedded within her living story. Her story forms an encapsulated worldview, and, as such, she has no reference point from which to observe the roles she acts out on a regular basis nor is there objectivity regarding the process of her living story. The counselor's responsibility is to help foster the client's ability to understand her living story, understand how the story came to be scripted for her, decide how she would like the story to be rescripted, and finally assist in the change process.

In this segment, the counselor is not satisfied that the full story has been articulated and shares an observation about the nature of what the client has labeled internal Sue. The counselor draws on the assessment of the client's core issues and coping style to share the idea that there is a loving and caring part (emotional deprivation) of Sue that holds back for fear of not being able to get it right (unrelenting standards). The client then gets in touch with a fear of failure about not meeting expectations and affirms the counselor's observation as accurate. From a core issue perspective, the counselor must be mindful to consider whether a third core issue is also present. Sue's mention of failure would suggest that the core issue of "failure" should also be considered.

Given the information gathered thus far, a core issue of failure is unlikely in that the feelings of failure are directly attached to, and result from, unrelenting standards. Nonetheless, the counselor must continue to hold this as a possibility and see if additional information comes forth in support of the hypothesis of a failure core issue.

The counselor then reflects back the three parts to the client and provides a frame that all of the parts exist within the client and in a sense take turns playing roles in her survival story. Recall that the survival story exists within the context of an "if-then" statement and is so deeply entrenched as a way of being in the world that the client continues to employ it as a strategy long after it has outlived its childhood usefulness. Because the survival story is no longer adaptively applicable to the client's current life, the story is seen as maladaptive in nature.

At this point in the interview, it is possible to establish a case conceptualization with some level of certainty. Sue's core issues and the process that unfolds in significant relational encounters with her husband are illustrated in Figure 5.1. This conceptualization involves the interplay of two different core issues that developed in childhood. Clearly Sue experienced emotional deprivation in her home environment. This lack of emotional connection created a personal hunger to be loved and to gain a sense of personal validation vis-à-vis her parents. Given that her parents were professionally focused, she attempted to win their approval, if not their affection, by responding with a compensation adaptation coping strategy, and in doing so she established the role of "Achieving Sue" who focused on her studies to the exclusion of social relationships. Another aspect of Sue's family life was the adherence to a rigid set of unrelenting standards. These standards served to establish a level of personal performance below which she should not fall. By the time Sue had met her husband, she had established an avoidance

FIGURE 5.1

Dynamic Interaction of Elements in the Client's Survival Story

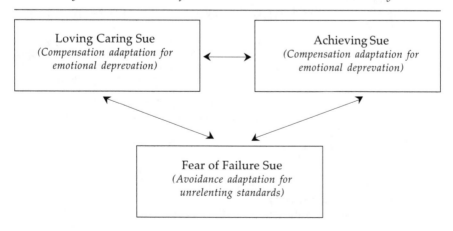

adaptation in response to her emotional deprivation core issue. That is, she avoided contact with others and even fought to keep from becoming further involved with her husband as he made attempts to court her early in their relationship. With some trepidation, Sue was able to push through the difficulty she had believing that someone could care for her and entered a relationship that later resulted in marriage. As time progressed and the relational connection began to become stressed, Sue's survival story and the core issues were triggered. Drawing on her early life experience, Sue feels that to be worthy of having someone care about her, she must perform to some set of standards she has created about being in a love relationship. This becomes problematic in that she also feels that she will never measure up to those standards, and fearing that she will disappoint her husband, she begins a process of avoiding further emotional connection. Employing this strategy, of course, sets the stage for further deterioration of the relationship and an increased sense of emotional deprivation. The story comes full circle and provides one more layer of validation for her relational worldview.

This scenario illustrates how the core issue story becomes a perpetual vicious cycle in a client's life. The manner in which the client responds to any one core issue tends to give the client exactly what is not wanted. In Sue's case, rather than deepening the emotional connection with her husband, she ends up feeling even more emotionally deprived. Only when Sue begins to recognize the manner in which she participates in her living story will her life begin to change as she makes different choices relative to that story. The next step is to have the client further externalize and objectify each part of her story. This can be done very effectively by helping the client to begin referencing each of the roles that have been established in the third person.

SEGMENT 13:
SUPPORTING THE MAJOR ROLES
IN THE CLIENT'S LIVING STORY

Counselor: So let's imagine that Achieving Sue came through the door and sat down here.

Sue: Uh, hum.

Counselor: What would you want to say to her relative to what you have just found out?

Sue: I guess I would say, I mean, the first thing I would want to say is, you know, I respect what you've done, and you have done some amazing things and you have achieved. That would be a really important thing to say to acknowledge the fact that these are achievements and they are something that she did.

Counselor: Uh, hum. And the other thing that really strikes me about her is that she really helped you all the way through your childhood.

Sue: She saved me.

Counselor: She sure did.

Sue: Yeah.

Counselor: Yeah. Uh, hum.

Sue: And so she's really important to me.

Counselor: Uh, hum. Good.

Sue: And I guess I would want her to know that too.

Counselor: Okay. Well let's have her sit on the side here, and now Loving Caring Sue comes in and sits down. What would you want to say to her?

Sue: That it's wonderful that you have the capacity to love and that you think about reaching out and that maybe, maybe you should do it more often. That those feelings are good. That maybe you should do it more often without feeling you're going to be rejected.

Counselor: Uh, hum.

Sue: And that just the fact that you do it is good; and if you're rejected, it's not the end of the world.

Counselor: Uh, hum. Okay. And I guess my sense, and what I would want to say to Loving Caring Sue, is that that is probably very difficult for her. That there was a point early in her life when she probably did want to express loving and caring and probably didn't get that in return.

Sue: Right.

Counselor: At least from what you have described as what happened with your mom and your dad.

Sue: Right.

Counselor: That as a child Loving Caring Sue really had no choice but to love and care, and not having that ever returned and nurtured must have been a very painful thing for her.

Sue: That's true. But there's still a part of me that wants to say, "Cut the shit, just let yourself say what you want to say, if you know you love someone, love someone, and get on with it."

Counselor: Okay.

Sue: I still think that's my external self.

Counselor: That really does sound like the Achieving Sue who is going to come in here and kind of say, you know, "Come on, let's snap it up."

Sue: Exactly.

Counselor: Okay. Well, let's put both of them kind of sitting next to one another in silence for the time. Now say Fear of Failure Sue comes through the door and sits there; what might be something that you'd like to say to her?

Sue: That's the Sue I just want to hold.

Counselor: You want to hold?

Sue: Say that it's okay. That there's a lot of things to be fearful of, life is full of things to be fearful of. But it's okay to be fearful.

Counselor: Uh, hum.

Sue: And the only way to deal with it is to kind of work through it and maybe to share those fears.

Counselor: Uh, hum.

Sue: Not keep repressing them and thinking that somehow I'm weak because I have those feelings.

Counselor: And I've labeled her Fear of Failure Sue.

Sue: Oh yeah.

Counselor: Is that the primary fear, or are there other fears as well?

Sue: That's the biggest.

Counselor: The biggest.

Sue: The biggest is fear of failure.

Counselor: Okay.

Sue: Fear of disappointing.

Counselor: Okay. Uh, hum. It almost sounds like fearful Sue needs to take on some responsibility for whether or not other people are going to be pleased with the outcomes.

Sue: Yeah. Oh yeah. Yeah, yeah, yeah.

Counselor: Okay, so it's not necessarily just you're own standards or her own standards, it's also the standards of other people that . . .

Sue: Absolutely. Absolutely.
Counselor: Okay. So failure not only in not accomplishing what the goals were but also failure around meeting other people's expectations?
Sue: Yup.
Counselor: Okay. All right.

Analysis of Segment 13

In this segment it can clearly be seen that offering support to the major roles of self that constitute the client's survival story is very important. For many clients, the parts that are the strongest and helped them survive are experienced as providing strength and safety. Making sure that each part is honored helps to ensure that the safety needed in going forward is in place (Parry & Doan, 1994). In this portion of the interview, the client states that it was Achieving Sue that saved her. This should give a clear indication to the counselor of how important that part of Sue is to her living story.

Providing attention to Loving Caring Sue begins the process of the client re-authoring her own living story. This is the part of Sue that needs to be nurtured. In many ways Loving Caring Sue establishes the leading edge of her growth and development. The origin of this part of Sue was in not having her emotional needs for love and affection adequately met as a child. Helping Sue give voice to this part of herself and to further validate this part provides a most favorable opportunity for a major transformation for her. As the client was beginning to explore this element of herself, it was very interesting to see that Achieving Sue barged back into the session. This is consistent with the client's old survival story. The counselor marks this event as an early indication of what a struggle it will be for the client to make the shift away from a worldview dominated by Achieving Sue to a worldview that is balanced with elements of Loving Caring Sue.

The other part of the client's story that originated from her emotional deprivation core issue has been labeled Fear of Failure Sue. In response to imagining fearful Sue and what causes the fear state, the client says, "This is the part that I just want to hold." Again, there is support for a core issue of emotional deprivation, but for the first time the client identifies what this part needs. It is interesting that Sue speaks about this part of herself in a manner similar to what she said she most needed from her mother in response to the miracle question posed earlier in the session. Finally, there is some clarification regarding the need to consider a core issue of failure versus the idea that Fear of Failure Sue is an artifact of emotional deprivation and unrelenting standards. The client states that what is most difficult for her is dealing with the "fear of disappointing." Although this could be seen as a failure core issue, the evidence so far suggests that it is much more consistent with an avoidance adaptation to an unrelenting standards core issue. Therefore, the existence of a legitimate third core issue of failure is not likely.

SEGMENT 14:
SUMMARIZING, SETTING A DIRECTION FOR CHANGE, AND RE-AUTHORING THE LIVING STORY

Counselor: Well, it sounds like there are three parts so far, and there may be more that might surface as time goes on for you. But I'm really curious as to which of those three parts you would like to kind of see become more prominent?

Sue: I, yeah, I want to be able to love.

Counselor: Okay, so that's the Loving Caring Sue?

Sue: Yup.

Counselor: Okay. All right.

Sue: Yup.

Counselor: Well, it seems like two different things need to happen to make that a reality. One would be to find ways in which Loving Caring Sue can visit you more often. The second element is to find ways that Loving Caring Sue can feel okay when Achieving Sue comes to visit at the same time. Is there ever a time when those two don't visit together?

Sue: When they don't visit?

Counselor: Yeah. I mean does one always stay away when the other is present?

Sue: Yeah. I don't think they like one another too much.

Counselor: They don't like one another.

Sue: Yeah, I don't think they're too compatible.

Counselor: So, what types of things would Loving Caring Sue need in order to manage the visits from Achieving Sue when she comes around?

Sue: I think that she needs to be strong enough to know that that loving part is a really beautiful part and a positive part.

Counselor: Uh, hum.

Sue: And that she has tremendous strength. And there is so much strength in being able to love.

Counselor: That's interesting to me because probably about 15 or 20 minutes ago you talked about the weakness of your more feeling side, and now you're talking about the great strength of that side.

Sue: Yeah.

Counselor: I'm really interested in that shift. Where did that come from?

Sue: Yeah. Well, I guess, you know, thinking about it and really being really honest with you and feeling comfortable and trusting you has sort of allowed me to open myself up to that idea.

Counselor: Uh, hum. And what kind of strengths are part of that side?

Counselor: I just, I mean, I guess the strength of being able to express you're feelings, of being able to have true friendships, of being able to give, of being able to actually feel that warmth inside—that realness.

Counselor: Uh, hum.

Sue: Yeah, it sounds very strong to me.

Counselor: Uh, hum.

Sue: And maybe I called it weak before, I mean it always has been. I've always looked at it as being weak.

Counselor: Uh, hum.

Sue: But also because, you know, I still don't know if I can do it and, so if I can't do it, and it's a good thing to do, then I screwed up again.

Counselor: Uh, hum. Okay. So I'm beginning to see a part of the process here. It seems like where there's a situation and Loving Caring Sue comes to visit there is a sense of strength and power there but also a sense that I need to do it right.

Sue: That's right.

Counselor: Which is Achieving Sue coming to visit.

Sue: That's right.

Counselor: And then once the two of them face off, Fear of Failure Sue comes in strengthening Achieving Sue's position and forcing Loving Caring Sue to back down.

Sue: I think, yes, that's very good, yup.

Counselor: Uh, hum. Okay. So I think one of the goals that might be useful is to think about ways in which you can allow Loving Caring Sue to build on her strengths and build on her coping strategies when these other two come to visit.

Sue: Hmmm.

Counselor: Now that is some work that you may or may not want to do down the road. But, if you can, just off the top of your head right now, what might be some coping strategies that Loving Caring Sue really needs to build as resources to help her cope with the situations when Achieving Sue and Fear of Failure Sue come to visit?

Sue: Well, I don't know, I suppose what's striking me most is that if Loving Caring Sue allows herself to come forward in spite of protestations from Achieving Sue and finds that the world doesn't end or there is reciprocal care, understanding and receives nurturing back, maybe that in itself will build on itself.

Counselor: Uh, hum.

Sue: That it's just a matter of taking risks, if you will, with that side and saying, "I can't control what happens; all I can do is control what I'm doing."

Counselor: Okay. So in the face of any number of obstacles for Loving Caring Sue, essentially she needs to be able to be resilient.

Sue: Right.

Counselor: To show courage to allow for the cycle to begin. It's almost like you were talking about a cycle of caring and then getting some nurturing back from showing that caring.

Sue: Uh, hum.

Counselor: Only right now Loving Caring Sue hasn't moved forward enough to allow for that cycle to begin that might nurture her and bring her back.

Sue: That's right, that's right.

Counselor: Okay. Great. Well, I've taken some of your time today, and I really want to thank you for coming in. But before we end, I'd just like to ask you to summarize a little bit about where you started from today, where you are now, and what you think might be some of the things you'd like to move toward in the future. Do you have a sense about that?

Sue: Yeah. I think I started today not knowing really what to expect.

Counselor: Uh, hum.

Sue: I have been in counseling for 6 months, but I think I started still believing and still accepting the fact that my feeling side was a really negative part of me.

Counselor: Uh, hum.

Sue: And that my achieving side was what was important and what I should incorporate into my entire being.

Counselor: Uh, hum.

Sue: I never admitted before about what I said to you about my mom.

Counselor: Uh, hum.

Sue: And I've just really wished that she would hold me.

Counselor: Uh, hum.

Sue: I feel good that I admitted that. I think that it's a big part, and I think that in and of itself sort of comes forth and makes me a more real person. Also, the fact that I'm able to admit that I need to be loved.

Counselor: Uh, hum.

Sue: And coming to the point where I really think that I do need to develop strengths. Strengths that are inside me . . .

Counselor: Uh, hum.

Sue: . . . to be able to reach out to others and to love without fear of rejection, fear of failure, to just let myself be a more real individual.

Counselor: Uh, hum. Okay. And in terms of the future, specifically where do you think you could begin, and where would you like it to go?

Sue: Well, the first thing I'd really like to do is go home and tell my husband I love him.

Counselor: Uh, hum.

Sue: And then tell him some of these things.

Counselor: Uh, hum.

Sue: And maybe it's time he knew who I am.

Counselor: Uh, hum. Okay.

Sue: And I really think that by working on that relationship, if I can share a lot of these things, I think I'll be able to carry it, you know, outside of just my relationship with him.

Counselor: Uh, hum. Uh, hum. Okay. It sounds like that is going to create a number of visits from Achieving Sue and Fear of Failure Sue.

Sue: Sure sounds like it, doesn't it? I know.

Counselor: What do you anticipate being some of the reactions from these other parts that come to visit at that time?

Sue: Yeah. Yeah, they'll react. And as I said, you know the Achieving Sue saved me, and I'm not ready to totally get rid of her.

Counselor: Uh, hum.

Sue: And I don't know, maybe it's the Loving Caring Sue that needs to nurture the Achieving Sue a little bit.

Counselor: Uh, hum.

Sue: Care about who she is, that will make them all sort of cohabit better than in the past.

Counselor: Right. Well, that sounds good. I would encourage you to continue to work with Martha on that and, if you wish to share anything that we talked about here, you know that would be fine. And please, if you will get in contact with me through Martha, just to let me know what has happened with you.

Sue: I will.

Counselor: And I wish you the best of luck.

Sue: Thanks.

Counselor: All right.

Analysis of Segment 14

This final segment of the interview involved three different elements. The first element was to have the client summarize material that was covered in the session. Asking the client to summarize her experience of the session allows the counselor to assess the degree to which the efforts put forth by the counselor were successful in meeting the goals for the session.

The second element was helping the client set a direction for change should she wish to work toward the goals she voiced as wanting to pursue. How does this client really want her life to be? She replies, "I want to be able to love." Over the course of the session, Loving Caring Sue was able to emerge with greater prominence and begin to become a voice in Sue's living story. The degree to which this part of the client's living story remains prominent is largely dependent on how successful the client is at continuing to make changes that are more adaptive.

As the various characters in Sue's living story are brought forth, the repetitive core issues process is clarified. Sue holds a deep need and desire for closeness in relationship with her husband. In part, the contextual aspect of this need is shaped by a compensation adaptation to the emotional deprivation she experienced as a child (see Figure 5.2).

As Loving Caring Sue reaches out, she does so with the idea that she meets a set of requirements that may be understood as her unrelenting standards. Holding these unrelenting standards triggers a level of fear and trepidation, giving rise to Fear of Failure Sue, as can be seen in Figure 5.3. When this happens, Achieving Sue emerges to take control to keep the threat of weakness of Fear of Failure Sue from placing the whole system at risk. The problem with this living story is that in responding to Fear of Failure Sue, Achieving Sue covers up or pushes out Loving Caring Sue, thereby destroying any hope of the client having her need for love and connection met in relationship with her husband.

The third element of this session was aimed at encouraging Sue to take on the process of re-authoring her living story and at the same time help her become aware of the obstacles that are likely to present themselves as she endeavors to make this change. Re-authoring a living story begins with addressing and changing the way that the characters, reflected as core issue roles, interact with each other. The interaction of the characters in the client's story reflects the core issues processes that are triggered in an effort to cope with each situation. The counselor used the term *visits* when referencing the emergence of various characters in Sue's living story. Parry and Doan (1994) suggest that framing parts as individual entities that visit in response to a situation is extremely helpful in getting the client to objectify and examine the parts of the self. This is a major goal in the process of deconstructing the story. Another component in this segment was the shift Sue makes from seeing the feeling aspects of her experiences as weaknesses to perceiving them as strengths.

FUTURE SESSIONS WITH SUE

As this case has shown, conducting a core issues assessment and employing the concept of narrative, as it is captured in the living story, can be an extremely useful aid in fostering an effective counseling intervention pro-

FIGURE 5.2

The Client's Motivation for Relationship Engagement

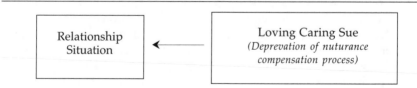

FIGURE 5.3

The Problematic Process of the Survival Story Feeding Forward in Adult Life

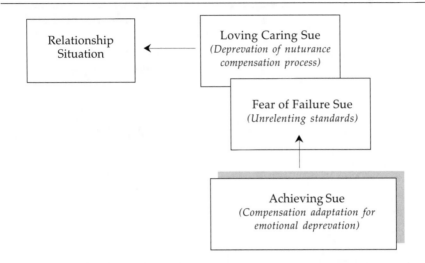

cess. Helping the client identify core issue struggles provides a way for the client to understand the problems that can interfere with finding greater satisfaction in his or her relationships with self, others, and the nature of the world. This was certainly the case for Sue. Sue's responses, especially later in the session, suggest that she is motivated to continue her work in counseling. Having the experience of engaging in a core issues assessment appears to have unlocked a level of understanding that heretofore had not been present. The next question must be, "Where do we go from here?"

From a narrative perspective, future sessions would involve assisting Sue in shifting away from living her old and out-of-date survival story and toward a new story that is more adaptive to her current situation and stage of life. Movement toward a new story will involve engaging Sue in a creative process that, in the end, will result in a re-authored living story. Sue will create this new story. Given the content of this session, the title of her re-authored and more adaptive new story might be "To Love Without Fear." The nature of this re-authored story, depicted in Figure 5.4, shows that Loving Caring Sue has now grown to be stronger and more prominent in her story role. She can no longer be totally covered up or pushed aside when Fear of Failure Sue and Achieving Sue come to visit.

The relative ease with which any client can make the types of changes that are ahead for Sue is highly dependent on a number of variables that come into play when examining the efficacy of counseling interventions. The work ahead of Sue is substantial and will draw on her level of commitment and her ability to muster directed effort to bring her desired state of relationship to fruition. From this point forward Sue will need to become more aware of her own process at points when her various core issues are triggered and she enters into living out her survival story.

FIGURE 5.4

A Possible Re-Authored Story That Allows the Client to Engage in a Relationship

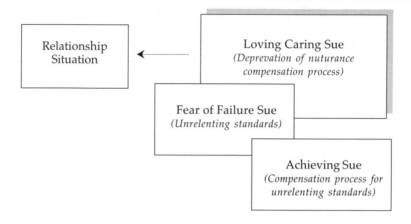

Following the process outlined in chapter 4, the counselor would continue to try to anticipate stress points and build the client's skill repertoire so that all aspects of the re-authored living story are given the best possible chance to become firmly established. The counselor would also track the nature of the obstacles Sue encounters as she begins to live out the changes inherent to her new story. Sue is bound to revert to the old story at some stress points during the process. Stress points in any process of client change are inevitable, and the counselor must help the client realize this fact and discuss it to help ensure that any relapses encountered are brief in nature.

SUMMARY

This chapter illustrates a core issues assessment with a client that used elements that emerged from that assessment to inform the direction of a counseling plan. Specific elements of the session were detailed as a means of demonstrating the various elements discussed in previous chapters. The nature of the client's core issues emerged over the course of the interview as a result of the counselor using a variety of techniques to probe for detail. One of the most striking features of this interview is the profound impact that identifying the core issue had on this client. Counselors who have worked with this model have reported similar results. When clients are able to formulate an understanding of how various elements of their relational histories have served to create specific beliefs about themselves, others, and the world, there is often an opening to consider alternative paths toward change. A video of this session is available through ACA Online Courses (www.counseling.org).

CHAPTER 6

Incorporating the Core Issues
Framework in Counseling Practice

■

This book offers counselors a means for formulating a better understanding of their clients during the counseling process. This
brief chapter provides some concluding thoughts on the model
and some of its limitations, considerations of the counselor's own
core issues, and the next steps that counselors might consider should
they wish to incorporate the core issues framework into practice.

■

The overall goal is to present a model that might help counselors think past
a symptom-based formulation for diagnosis and incorporate a structured
process for analyzing the vast amount of information clients reveal about
their struggles in life. Case study material was presented to show how this
model enables counselors to form deeper understandings of a client's problematic life themes as they relate to personal perceptions of self, others, and
the nature of the world. With this understanding in place, the counselor is
better able to assist clients not only in telling their own living story but also
in building a foundation for how that living story might become more consistent with clients' personal needs and desires.

It is not surprising, given the major influences of psychiatry and clinical
psychology, that the mental health industry has adopted a medically framed
and illness-based system as its standard for diagnosis. It is puzzling, however, given the counseling profession's rich history and the literature supporting the tenets of human development theories and models of intervention and
change, that counselors would limit their formal diagnostic assessment procedures to those associated with the traditional *DSM-IV-TR* psychiatric disorders. I believe assessment can be taken a step further to provide a more comprehensive and holistic basis for conceptualizing a client's struggle. Marriage
and family therapists have endorsed the idea of using relationally based models for assessment and diagnosis for many years (Kaslow, 1996). Engaging

systematically in a functional analysis of the relational family structure is a hallmark of the systems perspective. Assessing such elements as boundary permeability, expression of caring, articulation of feelings for others, acceptance of differences, sense of cooperation, and responding to the feeling of others all assist the clinician in understanding the overall level of functioning within the relational system (Watts, Trusty, & Lim, 1996). Clearly there is a place for a framework that helps us better understand the nature of individual client problems in a more holistic manner.

Clinical experience provides ample opportunity for counselors to discern the complexity involved when assessing the nature of client problems. It is often difficult to accurately pinpoint the portion of a client's informational content on which to focus a counseling intervention that will support client growth and decrease the likelihood of relapse. It would be extremely rare for a client to come into a counselor's office and begin the first session by stating, "I need help with a *relationship with other problem* that seems to result from my tendency to employ an *avoidant coping style* whenever my *emotional deprivation core issue* is triggered."

To arrive at an accurate assessment of the client's underlying problem, the counselor must listen for the salient portions of the client's report and compare that content with some plausible diagnostic template. Doing so will assist the counselor in determining the most appropriate focus for future sessions and suggest a manner in which to engage the client in co-constructing the short- and long-term goals for the overall counseling plan. Utilizing a core issues framework as a diagnostic template increases the probability that counselors will use more of the information gathered at intake and across counseling sessions as a means of systematically focusing their assessments and counseling intervention plans.

Because every perspective carries within it its own set of limitations, counselors would be wise to continue to build multiple perspectives for understanding the nature of the human condition across the full spectrum of human functioning. Although I strongly support the use of core issues as a basis for conceptualizing the nature of a client's struggle, I do not consider it a stand-alone system of assessment and diagnosis.

THE COUNSELOR'S CORE ISSUES

It is very likely that one or more of the issues described in previous chapters will be consistent with the counselor's own history and personal experience. In my many core issues workshops and in my work with counselors and graduate students in supervision, I have found this to be a very common experience. It is the rare person who has not suffered some form of relational wound that carries with it elements that have a lasting impact on one's perceptions of self, others, or the nature of the world. If you consider the important element of using the self as an instrument of change in the counseling process, it quickly becomes apparent that gaining clarity of your own core issues, how they are triggered, and the impact that they have in your personal and professional life is extremely important. Consider applying the core issues framework in your own supervision. The model also has great utility for supervisors who wish to employ it to help supervisees better understand the nature of thoughts, feelings, and in-session behaviors triggered by their clients.

LEARN THE ELEMENTS OF
THE CLIENT CORE ISSUES MODEL

Counselors must be thoroughly familiar with the nature of the model they use to conduct diagnostic assessments. Clients are never well served if their counselors do not know what they are doing. Learning to recognize each of the core issues and how each is expressed by virtue of the three coping process styles is a first necessary step before employing this model in practice. Repeatedly reviewing the information presented in earlier chapters will help you build a knowledge base of the core issues framework.

As counselors become increasingly familiar with the content and nature of the model, it is useful to engage in a core issues case file review and analysis exercise. Examine the intake assessments and case notes of previous clients for evidence of one or more core issues and their associated coping processes. Once the core issue hypothesis is formed, look through the case notes for evidence that would support or invalidate that hypothesis. This exercise provides a great opportunity to gain familiarity with how client information is used in arriving at a core issues determination during the assessment phase of the counseling process.

Once you have built some confidence on paper, the next step is to apply it during the assessment phase with clients. Assuming you already have experience conducting a full biopsychosocial intake interview, much of the initial information needed for a preliminary core issues assessment can be gathered by simply completing that interview process. What will likely be missing at this point is the ability to probe crisply for historical content to first reach initial core issue hypotheses and later to discover the information that lends validity to those hypotheses. As you gain experience in the assessment process, greater cognitive elasticity in specifically probing core issue information will result. The most important element during this phase of learning is to engage in repetitive practice with clients in-session and to review the core issues material on a regular basis. The biggest mistake I see graduate students make when learning this process is being much too eager to arrive at a conclusion. Careful consideration of all the information available is critically important.

Forming a consultation group composed of individuals interested in working from a core issues model can be very valuable in helping to ensure accuracy of a core issue assessment. It is important to remember that the counseling process is greatly aided when the counseling intervention is focused on the correct core issue. The opposite is also true. If the counselor focuses on the wrong core issue, it will not resonate with the client's experience and will fail to access the affect associated with the client's struggle. In such cases the process stalls and often hits a dead end. Therefore, engaging in discussions about the use of the core issues model with a supervisor and other counselors with whom you consult can be an extremely valuable asset during this phase of professional development.

Although the core issues framework illustrated in Chapter 5 was based largely on concepts associated with cognitive theory, the manner in which you address the issues that emerge in the assessment is open to any type of intervention with which you are most comfortable. In the preceding chapters I have presented some of the advantages of having an established complementary framework to use in assessing the broader problematic themes that are consistently expressed by clients as they report the nature of their struggles in life.

Keep in mind that we are all living out our own narrative on a daily basis. This framework provides a means for understanding the nature of that living story as it exists in the past as well as in the present. The living story also provides a means for understanding how one's narrative might be transformed. This transformation is best brought about by helping the client to understand the old strategies once used to survive in life and move past them to consider how the client might create a new living story—a story that supports a life based not on the need to survive but rather on a life from which one will thrive!

References

American Psychiatric Association. (1952). *Diagnostic and statistical manual.* Washington, DC: Author.

American Psychiatric Association. (2000). *Diagnostic and statistical manual* (4th ed., text revision). Washington, DC: Author.

Antony, M., & Barlow, D. H. (Eds.). (2001). *The handbook of assessment and treatment planning for psychological disorders.* New York: Guilford Press.

Babrow, A. S., Kline, K. N., & Rawlins, W. K. (2005). Narrating problems and problematizing narratives: Linking problematic integration and narrative theory in telling *stories* about our health. In L. M. Hater, P. M. Japp, & C. S. Beck (Eds.), *Narratives, health, and healing: Communication theory, research, and practice* (pp. 31–52). Mahwah, NJ: Lawrence Erlbaum.

Ball, J., Mitchell, P., & Malhi, G. (2003). Schema-focused cognitive therapy for bipolar disorder: Reducing vulnerability to relapse through attitudinal change. *Australian and New Zealand Journal of Psychiatry, 37,* 41–48.

Barnes, K. L. (2003). Review of *Counseling across the lifespan: Prevention and treatment. Counselor Education and Supervision, 43,* 78–80.

Beck, A. T. (1967). *Depression: Causes and treatment.* Philadelphia: University of Pennsylvania Press.

Beck, A. T., Rush, A. J., Shaw, B. R., & Emery, G. (1979). *Cognitive therapy of depression.* New York: Guilford Press.

Beck, A.T., & Weishaar, M. (1989). Cognitive therapy. In A. Freeman, K. M. Simon, L. E. Beutler, & H. Arkowitz (Eds.), *Comprehensive handbook of cognitive therapy* (pp. 21–36). New York: Plenum.

Beck, A. T., & Young, J. E. (1985). Depression. In D. H. Barlow (Ed.), *Clinical handbook of psychological disorders: A step-by-step treatment manual* (pp. 206–244). New York: Guilford Press.

Berg, A. (1991). Genograms, generalizability, quantities and qualities. *Journal of the American Board of Family Practice, 4,* 468–469.

Berg, I., & Miller, S. (1992). *Working with the problem drinker.* New York: Norton.

Britton, J. (1982). *Prospect and retrospect: Selected essays of James Britton.* Portsmouth, NH: Boynton/Cook.

Bruner, J. (1990). *Acts of meaning.* Cambridge, MA: Harvard University Press.

Burke, J. F. (1989). *Contemporary approaches to psychotherapy and counseling: The self-regulation and maturity model.* Pacific Grove, CA: Brooks/Cole.

Carnevale, J. P. (1989). *Counseling gems: Thought for the practitioner.* Muncie, IN: Accelerated Development.

Carver, C. S., Scheier, M. F., & Weintraub, J. K. (1989). Assessing coping strategies: A theoretically based approach. *Journal of Personality and Social Psychology, 56,* 267–283.

Catford, L., & Ray, M. (1991). *The path of the everyday hero: Drawing on the power of myth to meet life's most important challenges.* Los Angeles, CA: Jeremy P. Tarcher.

Cecero, J. J., & Young, J. E. (2001). Case of Silvia: A schema focused approach. *Journal of Psychotherapy Integration, 11,* 217–229.

Chu, J. A. (1992). The therapeutic roller coaster: Dilemmas in the treatment of childhood abuse survivors. *Journal of Psychotherapy Practice and Research, 1,* 351–370.

Comas-Diaz, L. (1996). Cultural considerations in diagnosis. In F. W. Kaslow (Ed.), *Handbook of relational diagnosis and dysfunctional family patterns* (pp. 152–170). New York: Wiley.

Corey, G., Corey, M., & Callanan, P. (2007). *Issues and ethics in the helping professions* (7th ed.). Pacific Grove, CA: Thomson Brooks/Cole.

de Shazer, S. (1988). *Clues: Investigating solutions in brief therapy.* New York: Norton.

Erikson, E. (1963). *Childhood and society.* New York: Norton.

Everly, G. S., & Lating, J. M. (2004). Personality-guided therapy for posttraumatic stress disorder. In *Personality-guided psychology* (pp. 33–51). Washington, DC: American Psychological Association.

Flanagan, C. M. (1993). Treating neurotic problems that do not respond to psychodynamic therapies. *Hospital and Community Psychiatry, 44,* 824–826.

Gladstone, A. (1955). Threats and response to threats. *Bulletin of the Research Exchange on the Prevention of War, 3,* 23–31.

Goldfried, M. (2003). Cognitive-behavioral therapy: Reflections on the evolution of a therapeutic orientation. *Cognitive Therapy and Research, 27,* 53–69.

Grossmann, K. E., Grossmann, K., & Keppler, A. (2005). Universal and culture-specific aspects of human behavior: The case of attachment. In W. Friedlmeier, P. Chakkarath, & B. Schwarz (Eds.), *Culture and human development: The importance of cross-cultural research for the social sciences* (pp. 75–97). Hove, England: Psychology Press/Erlbaum (UK) Taylor & Francis.

Halliday, M.A. (1989). *Spoken and written language.* Oxford: Oxford University Press.

Halstead, R. W. (1996). The assessment and treatment of relationship wounds. *The Hatherleigh guide to issues in modern therapy* (pp. 177–200). New York: Hatherleigh Press.

Hardy, B. (1977). Narrative as a primary act of the mind. In M. Meek, A. Warlow, & G. Barton (Eds.), *The cool web: The pattern of children's learning* (pp. 12–23). London: Bodley Head.

Herman, J. (1992). *Trauma and recovery.* New York: Basic Books.

Hoffart, A., Versland, S., & Sexton, H. (2002). Self-understanding, empathy, guided discovery, and schema belief in schema-focused cognitive therapy of personality problems: A process-outcome study. *Cognitive Therapy and Research, 26,* 199–212.

Horvath, A. O., & Greenberg, L. S. (1987). The development of the working alliance inventory. In L. S. Greenberg & W. M. Pinsof (Eds.), *The psychotherapeutic research process: A research handbook* (pp. 529–556). New York: Guilford Press.

Howard, G. (1989). A tale of two stories: Excursions into a narrative approach to psychology and psychotherapy. *American Psychologist, 46,* 187–197.

Ibrahim, F., Roysircar-Sodowsky, G., & Ohnishi, H. (2001). Worldview. In J. G. Ponterotto, J. M. Casas, L. A. Suzuki, & C. M. Alexandra (Eds.), *Handbook of multicultural counseling* (pp. 425–456). Thousand Oaks, CA: Sage.

Kaslow, F. (1996). History, rationale, and philosophic overview of issues and assumptions of relational diagnosis. In F. W. Kaslow (Ed.), *Handbook of relational diagnosis and dysfunctional family patterns* (pp. 3–18). New York: Wiley.

Kegan, R. (1982). *The evolving self.* Cambridge, MA: Harvard University Press.

Kihlstrom, J. (2002). To honor Kraepelin: From symptoms to pathology in the diagnosis of mental illness. In L. Beutler & M. Malkik (Eds.), *Rethinking the DSM: A psychological perspective.* Washington, DC: American Psychological Association.

Lane, B. (1993). *Writing as a road to self-recovery.* Cincinnati, OH: Writer's Digest Books.

Lazarus, R. S. (1991). *Emotion and adaptation.* New York: Oxford University Press.

Lazarus, R. S., & Folkman, S. (1984). *Stress, appraisal, and coping.* New York: Springer.

Lee, C. W., Taylor, G., & Dunn, J. (1999). Factor structure of the Schema Questionnaire in a large clinical sample. *Cognitive Therapy and Research, 23,* 441–451.

Levitt, J. T., Hoffman, E. C., Grisham, J. R., & Barlow, D. H. (2001). Empirically supported treatments for panic disorder. *Psychiatric Annals, 3,* 478–487.

Madden, R. G. (1998). *Legal issues in social work, counseling, and mental health: Guidelines for clinical practice in psychotherapy.* Thousand Oaks, CA: Sage.

Maslow, A. (1971). *The farther reaches of human nature.* New York: Harmondworth.

McGoldrick, M., Gerson, R., & Shellenberger, S. (1999). *Genograms: Assessment and intervention.* New York: Norton.

McHale, B. (1992). *Constructing postmodernism.* London: Routledge.

Morrison, N. (2000). Schema-focused cognitive therapy for complex long-standing problems: A single case study. *Behavioral and Cognitive Therapy, 28,* 269–283.

Nussbaum, P. (1988). Narrative emotion: Beckett's genealogy of love. In S. Hauerwas & L. G. Jones (Eds.), *Why narrative? Readings in narrative theology* (pp. 41–78). Grand Rapids, MI: William B. Eerdmans.

Parry, A., & Doan, R. (1994). *Story re-visions: Narrative therapy in the postmodern world.* New York: Guilford Press.

Pedersen, P. (2001). Mobilizing the generic potential of culture-centered counseling. *International Journal for the Advancement of Counseling, 23,*165–177.

Perry, W. (1970). *Forms of intellectual and ethical development in the college years: A scheme.* New York: Holt, Rinehart, & Winston.

Piaget, J. (1969). *The psychology of the child.* New York: Wiley.

Polkinghorne, D. (1988). *Narrative knowing and the human sciences.* Albany, NY: State University of New York Press.

Ramsay, J. R. (1998). Postmodern cognitive therapy: Cognitions, narratives, and personal meaning-making. *Journal of Cognitive Psychotherapy, 12*(1), 39–55.

Ricoeur, P. (1984). *Time and narrative* (Vol. 1). Chicago: University of Chicago Press.

Schmidt, N. B., Joiner, T. E., Young, J. E., & Telch, M. J. (1995). The Schema Questionnaire: Investigation of psychometric properties and the hierarchical structure of a measure of maladaptive schemas. *Cognitive Therapy and Research, 19,* 295–321.

Seligman, M. E. (1975). *Helplessness: On depression, development, and death.* Oxford, England: W. H. Freeman.

Seligman, M. E., & Csikszentmihalyi, M. (2000). Positive psychology: An introduction. *American Psychologist, 55,* 5–14.

Sharf, R. (2003). *Theories of psychotherapy and counseling* (5th ed.). Pacific Grove, CA: Brooks/Cole.

Shea, S. C. (1998). *Psychiatric interviewing: The art of understanding.* Philadelphia, PA: W. B. Saunders.

Spence, D. P. (2003). Listening for rhetorical truth. *Psychoanalytic Quarterly, 74,* 875–903.

Staub, E. (1999). The roots of evil: Social conditions, culture, personality, and basic human needs. *Personality and Social Psychology Review, 3,* 179–192.

Sue, D. W., & Sue, D. (2003). *Counseling the culturally diverse: Theory and practice* (4th ed.) New York: Wiley.

Wadsworth, B. J. (1971). *Piaget's theory of cognitive development.* New York: David McKay.

Wanner, S. (1994). *On with the story: Adolescents learning through narrative.* Plymouth, NH: Boynton/Cole.

Watts, R. E., Trusty, J., & Lim, M. (1996). Characteristics of healthy families as a model of systemic social interest. *Canadian Journal of Adlerian Psychology, 26,* 1–12.

White, M. (1986). Negative explanation, restraint, and double description: A template for family therapy. *Family Process, 25,* 169–184.

White, M., & Epston, D. (1990). *Narrative means to therapeutic ends.* New York: Norton.

Witherell, C., & Noddings, N. (Eds.). (1991). *Stories lives tell: Narrative and dialog in education.* New York: Teachers College Press.

Wrosch, C., Scheier, M. F., Carver, C. S., & Schulz, R. (2003). The importance of goal disengagement in adaptive self-regulation: When giving up is beneficial. *Self & Identity, 2,* 1–20.

Young, J. E. (1990). *Cognitive therapy for personality disorders: A schema-focused approach.* Sarasota, FL: Professional Resource Press.

Young, J. E. (1999). *Cognitive therapy for personality disorders: A schema-focused approach* (2nd ed). Sarasota, FL: Professional Resource Press.

Young, J. E., Beck, A. T., & Weinberger, A. (1994). Depression. In D. H. Barlow (Ed.), *Clinical handbook of psychological disorders* (2nd ed., pp. 240–277). New York: Guilford Press.

Young, J. E., & Flanagan, C. (1998). Schema-focused therapy for narcissistic patients. In E. F Ronningstam (Ed.), *Disorders of narcissism: Diagnostic, clinical, and empirical implications* (pp. 239–262). Washington, DC: American Psychiatric Association.

Young, J. E., & Gluhoski, V. (1997). A schema-focused perspective on satisfaction in close relationships. In R. Sternberg & M. Hojjat (Eds.), *Satisfaction in close relationships* (pp. 356–381). New York: Guilford Press.

Young. J. E., Klosko, J. S., & Weishaar, M. (2003). *Schema therapy: A practitioner's guide.* New York: Gilford Press.

Young, J. E., & Mattila, D. (2002). Schema focused therapy for depression. In M. A. Reinecke & M. R. Davison (Eds.), *Comparative treatments of depression* (pp. 292–316). New York: Springer.

Young, J. E., Weinberger, A., & Beck, A. T. (2001). Depression. In D. H. Barlow (Ed.), *Clinical handbook of psychological disorders* (3rd ed., pp. 264–308). New York: Guilford Press.

Zuckerman, M., & Gagne, M. (2003). The COPE revised: Proposing a 5-factor model of coping strategies. *Journal of Research in Personality Assessment, 37,* 169–204.

Index

relational schema, 15
    maladaptive, 20–22
relational triad, 17–18, 32

Scheier, M. F., 11, 38, 39
schema, concept of, 14–15
    early maladaptive schema
        and core issues, 15–17,
        24–28
    maladaptive relational
        schema, 20–22
    worldview and, 15
    Young's schema domains,
        19–20
Schulz, R., 39
secondary appraisal process,
    coping and, 11
Seligman, M. E., 6, 38
stabilization and reduction of
    client symptoms, 4–5
Staub, E., 12
stories, client's living. *See* core
    issues stories
Stress/Threat Model of Coping,
    10–11
surrender adaptation, 38–39, 40

trauma, 9

Wadsworth, B. J., 15
Wanner, S., 56
Weintraub, J. K., 11, 38
Weishaar, M., 15, 16, 37, 38
White, M., 62
worldview, cognitive schema and,
    15
Wrosch, C., 39

Young, J. E., 34, 37, 58, 74
    coping response styles, 38,
        39
    core emotional needs, 12, 13,
        14, 16, 19
    Early Maladaptive Schema
        Framework, 16, 20,
        24–28
    relationally based diagnostic
        framework, 7
    schema domains, 19–20

Zuckerman, M., 38